CAPPADOCIA INSIDER'S TRAVEL GUIDE

HAMID ABEL

Copyright © 2024 by *Hamid Abel*

All rights reserved. No part of this publication may be reproduced, stored or transmitted in any form or by any means, electronic, mechanical, photocopying, recording, scanning, or otherwise without written permission from the publisher. It is illegal to copy this book, post it to a website, or distribute it by any other means without permission.

First edition 2024

Published by *Knowvelty Press*

CONTENTS

Introduction to Cappadocia 7

    OVERVIEW 7

    BRIEF HISTORY 10

    GEOGRAPHY AND CLIMATE....................................14

    LOCAL INSIGHTS: STORIES AND INTERVIEWS FROM CAPPADOCIAN RESIDENTS 17

Getting to Cappadocia 22

    TRANSPORTATION OPTIONS 22

    AIRPORTS AND AIRLINES 27

    LOCAL PHRASES & LANGUAGE GUIDE....................35

Where to Stay in Cappadocia 39

    ACCOMMODATION OPTIONS................................39

    CAVE HOTELS AND BOUTIQUE STAYS 44

    BUDGET, MID-RANGE, AND LUXURY OPTIONS........49

    LOCAL INSIGHTS: RECOMMENDATIONS FROM LOCALS ON HIDDEN GEMS FOR ACCOMMODATION 54

Exploring Cappadocia's Highlights 59

    GOREME OPEN-AIR MUSEUM...............................59

    FAIRY CHIMNEYS OF PASABAG VALLEY 64

    HOT AIR BALLOON RIDES 69

    LOVE VALLEY AND ROSE VALLEY............................74

UCHISAR CASTLE 78

LOCAL INSIGHTS: PHOTOGRAPHER'S PERSPECTIVE - PHOTOGRAPHY TIPS FOR CAPTURING CAPPADOCIA'S BEAUTY 83

Outdoor Activities in Cappadocia 89

HIKING AND TREKKING TRAILS...............................89

CYCLING ROUTES 94

LOCAL INSIGHTS: ADVENTURE STORIES AND RECOMMENDED OUTDOOR EXPERIENCES BY LOCALS 98

Cappadocian Cuisine and Dining Experiences ... 103

TRADITIONAL TURKISH CUISINE 103

LOCAL SPECIALTIES AND DISHES TO TRY 108

BEST RESTAURANTS AND CAFES IN CAPPADOCIA' 113

LOCAL INSIGHTS: FOOD STORIES AND FAVORITE DINING SPOTS SHARED BY LOCALS 117

Shopping in Cappadocia 122

SOUVENIRS AND HANDICRAFTS 122

POTTERY AND CERAMICS.....................................127

CARPETS AND TEXTILES 132

LOCAL INSIGHTS: ARTISANS' STORIES AND INSIDER TIPS ON WHERE TO FIND AUTHENTIC LOCAL CRAFTS 137

Cultural Experiences and Festivals 143

FOLK MUSIC AND DANCE PERFORMANCES 143

POTTERY WORKSHOPS 148

CAPPADOCIA FESTIVALS AND EVENTS 153

LOCAL INSIGHTS: CULTURAL STORIES AND
INTERVIEWS WITH ARTISTS AND PERFORMERS ... 158

Practical Tips for Traveling in Cappadocia 163

ESSENTIAL PACKING LIST 163

Safety Tips 169

LOCAL ETIQUETTE AND CUSTOMS 169

Day Trips and Excursions from Cappadocia 177

IHLARA VALLEY 177

SOGANLI VALLEY 186

MOUNT ERCIYES SKI RESORT 190

Sustainable Tourism in Cappadocia 199

RESPONSIBLE TRAVEL PRACTICES 199

ECO-FRIENDLY TOURS AND ACTIVITIES 204

SUPPORTING LOCAL COMMUNITIES 209

Additional Resources 214

MAPS OF CAPPADOCIA 214

LOCAL INSIGHTS: INSIDER TIPS AND RESOURCES
RECOMMENDED BY LOCALS 228

Introduction to Cappadocia

OVERVIEW

Nestled in the heart of Turkey, Cappadocia is a region unlike any other. Its surreal landscapes, dotted with fairy chimneys and ancient cave dwellings, evoke a sense of wonder and enchantment that captivates visitors from around the globe.

The story of Cappadocia begins millions of years ago, with the eruption of nearby volcanoes blanketing the region in thick layers of ash and lava. Over time, wind and water sculpted the soft volcanic rock into the otherworldly formations that define the Cappadocian landscape today. From towering rock pillars to honeycombed hillsides, every corner of Cappadocia seems like a scene from a fantasy novel brought to life.

But Cappadocia is more than just its natural wonders; it's also a region steeped in history and culture. For centuries, it has been a crossroads of civilizations, from the ancient Hittites to the Byzantines and Ottomans. This rich tapestry of heritage is reflected in the region's countless archaeological sites, including underground cities, rock-cut churches, and troglodyte villages carved into the soft tufa rock.

One of the most iconic features of Cappadocia is its cave dwellings. For millennia, people have carved homes, churches, and even entire cities into the soft volcanic rock, creating a labyrinth of tunnels and chambers that stretch for miles underground. Exploring these underground cities offers a glimpse into the ingenuity and resilience of the people who once called Cappadocia home.

But perhaps the most enchanting aspect of Cappadocia is its sense of timelessness. As the sun rises over the horizon, casting a warm glow across the rugged landscape, it's easy to feel as though you've stepped back in time to a world untouched by modernity. Whether you're soaring above the fairy chimneys in a hot air balloon, wandering through the winding streets of a cave village, or sipping tea with locals in a traditional Turkish cafe, Cappadocia has a way of captivating the imagination and leaving a lasting impression on all who visit.

In the pages of this guide, we'll delve deeper into the wonders of Cappadocia, exploring its hidden gems, uncovering its ancient mysteries, and sharing practical tips for making the most of your visit to this magical land. So pack your bags, prepare to be amazed, and get ready for the adventure of a lifetime in Cappadocia.

BRIEF HISTORY

To truly appreciate the enchanting landscapes and ancient wonders of Cappadocia, one must delve into its rich and storied history. From the dawn of civilization to the present day, the region has been shaped by countless cultures, conflicts, and conquests, leaving behind a legacy that is as diverse as it is fascinating.

The history of Cappadocia dates back thousands of years, with evidence of human habitation stretching back to the Paleolithic era. However, it was during the Bronze Age that the region began to flourish, with the emergence of the Hittite civilization around 1800 BCE. The Hittites established a powerful empire in central Anatolia, leaving behind impressive fortifications and monumental rock reliefs that still stand today.

In the centuries that followed, Cappadocia became a melting pot of cultures and civilizations, as successive waves of conquerors, including the Assyrians, Persians, and Greeks, vied for control of the region. However, it was the arrival of the Romans in the 1st century BCE that would leave the most enduring mark on Cappadocia's landscape.

Under Roman rule, Cappadocia flourished as a prosperous and strategically important province, thanks in part to its location along the Silk Road trade route. The Romans built numerous cities, roads, and fortifications throughout the region, many of which can still be seen today. However, it was also during this time that Christianity began to take root in Cappadocia, leading to the construction of countless rock-cut churches and monasteries hidden away in the region's rocky valleys.

In the centuries that followed, Cappadocia continued to be shaped by waves of conquest and migration, including the arrival of the Byzantines, Arabs, and Seljuks. Each successive culture left its own indelible mark on the region, from the elaborately decorated frescoes of the Byzantine churches to the towering minarets of the Seljuk mosques.

However, it was not until the 20th century that Cappadocia's modern identity began to take shape. Following the collapse of the Ottoman Empire, the region became part of the newly established Republic of Turkey. In the decades that followed, Cappadocia underwent rapid modernization and development, yet its ancient heritage remains as vibrant and captivating as ever.

Today, Cappadocia stands as a testament to the enduring spirit of human creativity and resilience. Its otherworldly landscapes, ancient ruins, and rich cultural heritage continue to draw visitors from around the world, inviting them to unravel the mysteries of the past and experience the magic of this timeless land for themselves.

GEOGRAPHY AND CLIMATE

Nestled in the heart of Anatolia, Cappadocia boasts a landscape that is as diverse as it is mesmerizing. From towering rock formations to lush valleys and fertile plains, the region's geography is a testament to the forces of nature and the passage of time.

At the heart of Cappadocia's landscape are its iconic fairy chimneys, towering pillars of rock that have been sculpted over millions of years by wind and water erosion. These surreal formations, with their whimsical shapes and honeycombed interiors, are a defining feature of the region and a source of endless fascination for visitors.

Surrounding the fairy chimneys are expansive valleys and canyons, carved into the soft volcanic rock by ancient rivers and streams. From the lush greenery of the Ihlara Valley to the rugged beauty of the Rose and Love Valleys, each valley offers its own unique blend of natural wonders and cultural treasures waiting to be discovered.

In addition to its valleys and rock formations, Cappadocia is also home to a network of underground cities, carved deep into the earth by ancient inhabitants seeking refuge from invaders and natural disasters. These subterranean labyrinths, with their intricate passageways and hidden chambers, provide a fascinating glimpse into the region's rich history and the ingenuity of its people.

Despite its arid climate, Cappadocia is also blessed with a wealth of natural resources, including fertile soil and abundant water sources. This has made the region a haven for agriculture since ancient times, with vineyards, orchards, and fields of wheat and barley stretching as far as the eye can see.

In terms of climate, Cappadocia experiences hot, dry summers and cold, snowy winters, with temperatures ranging from scorching highs in the summer to freezing lows in the winter. The best times to visit are in the spring and fall, when the weather is mild and the landscapes are at their most vibrant.

Whether you're exploring the otherworldly landscapes of the Fairy Chimney Valley, hiking through the lush greenery of the Rose Valley, or descending into the depths of an underground city, Cappadocia offers a wealth of natural wonders waiting to be discovered. So pack your bags, lace up your hiking boots, and get ready to embark on an unforgettable journey through this captivating land.

LOCAL INSIGHTS: STORIES AND INTERVIEWS FROM CAPPADOCIAN RESIDENTS

In the heart of Cappadocia lies not just a land of captivating landscapes and ancient wonders, but also a community of warm-hearted and hospitable locals who have called this region home for generations. To truly understand the essence of Cappadocia, one must listen to the stories and insights shared by its residents, whose lives are intertwined with the rich tapestry of history and culture that defines the region.

Ali, the Cave Dweller:

Ali, a jovial man with a twinkle in his eye, welcomes visitors to his cave dwelling with open arms and a warm smile. For Ali, living in a cave isn't just a matter of necessity; it's a way of life that connects him to the land and its ancient heritage.

"My family has lived in this cave for generations," he says proudly, gesturing to the rough-hewn walls and cozy alcoves that make up his home. "It's a part of who we are, a reminder of our ancestors and the resilience of the human spirit."

As Ali serves tea and shares stories of his childhood spent exploring the rocky hillsides of Cappadocia, it becomes clear that for him, home is more than just a place; it's a living, breathing entity that has shaped his identity and sense of belonging. "Every rock, every crevice tells a story," he muses, his eyes sparkling with nostalgia. "To live here is to be a part of something greater than oneself, to be connected to the land and its secrets."

Ayşe, the Keeper of Traditions:

In the bustling town of Göreme, Ayşe can be found tending to her family's pottery workshop, where she carries on the ancient craft that has been passed down through generations. For Ayşe, pottery isn't just a livelihood; it's a passion and a connection to her cultural heritage. "Our pottery tells the story of Cappadocia," she explains, her hands deftly shaping a lump of clay into a graceful vase. "Each piece is a reflection of the land and its people, a testament to our creativity and resilience."

As Ayşe shares the secrets of her craft, from the intricate designs inspired by the region's natural beauty to the time-honored techniques passed down from her ancestors, it becomes clear that pottery is more than just an art form; it's a way of preserving traditions and fostering a sense of community. "In a world that's constantly changing, pottery grounds us in the past while giving us hope for the future," she says with a smile, her hands still busy shaping the clay. "It's a reminder that no matter how far we may roam, Cappadocia will always be our home."

Mehmet, the Guardian of History:

As the sun sets over the ancient city of Kaymaklı, Mehmet stands watch over the labyrinthine tunnels and chambers that lie hidden beneath the earth. As a guide at the Kaymaklı Underground City, Mehmet has spent countless hours exploring its darkened passageways and unraveling the mysteries of its past. "This city is a testament to the ingenuity of our ancestors," he says, his voice echoing in the cavernous space. "They carved these tunnels with nothing but hand tools and sheer determination, creating a refuge that could withstand any threat."

As Mehmet leads visitors through the underground maze, pointing out the ancient kitchens, sleeping quarters, and churches that lie hidden beneath the surface, it becomes clear that for him, this is more than just a job; it's a calling and a responsibility. "We are the guardians of this history," he says solemnly, his gaze sweeping over the ancient stone walls. "It's our duty to ensure that future generations can learn from the past and carry on the legacy of Cappadocia."

In the voices and stories of Ali, Ayşe, Mehmet, and countless others, we glimpse the soul of Cappadocia – a land where tradition and innovation, history and hospitality, are woven together in a tapestry of life that is as vibrant and captivating as the landscapes that surround it. As we journey through this ancient land, let us not only marvel at its wonders but also take the time to listen to the voices of its people, whose stories are as enduring and unforgettable as the land itself.

Getting to Cappadocia

TRANSPORTATION OPTIONS

In a region as diverse and captivating as Cappadocia, getting around is an adventure in itself. From ancient cave villages to towering rock formations, there's no shortage of wonders to explore, and fortunately, there are plenty of transportation options to help you make the most of your journey.

1. Car Rental:

For those who prefer to chart their own course and explore at their own pace, renting a car is an excellent option. Cappadocia's well-maintained roads and scenic routes make for a delightful driving experience, allowing you to venture off the beaten path and discover hidden gems along the way. Rental agencies can be found in major towns and cities throughout the region, and a valid driver's license is typically all that's required to get behind the wheel.

2. Public Transportation:

For travelers looking to immerse themselves in the local culture and connect with the community, public transportation is a convenient and affordable option. Buses and dolmuş (shared taxis) are the most common modes of public transit in Cappadocia, with routes connecting major towns and attractions throughout the region. Whether you're traveling from Göreme to Uçhisar or exploring the ancient streets of Avanos, public transportation offers a convenient way to get around while mingling with locals along the way.

3. Guided Tours:

For those who prefer a more structured approach to exploration, guided tours are an excellent way to experience the highlights of Cappadocia with the expertise of a knowledgeable local guide. Whether you're embarking on a hot air balloon ride over the fairy chimneys, hiking through the picturesque valleys, or exploring the ancient underground cities, guided tours offer a hassle-free way to see the sights and learn about the region's history and culture along the way.

4. Bicycle Rentals:

For the adventurous souls who crave a more active way to explore Cappadocia's stunning landscapes, bicycle rentals are a popular choice. With miles of scenic trails and winding country roads to explore, cycling offers a unique perspective on the region's natural beauty, allowing you to soak in the sights and sounds at your own pace. Rental shops can be found in major towns and villages throughout Cappadocia, and guided cycling tours are also available for those looking for a more structured experience.

5. Horseback Riding:

For a truly unforgettable way to experience Cappadocia's rugged terrain, why not saddle up and explore on horseback? Horseback riding tours offer a unique perspective on the region's natural wonders, allowing you to traverse ancient trails, meander through verdant valleys, and soak in the panoramic views from atop your trusty steed. Whether you're a seasoned equestrian or a novice rider, there's a horseback riding tour to suit every skill level and interest.

6. Taxi Services:

For travelers seeking convenience and flexibility, taxi services are readily available throughout Cappadocia. Whether you need a ride to the airport, a lift to a nearby attraction, or a guided tour of the region's highlights, taxis offer a convenient and hassle-free way to get around. Many hotels and guesthouses can arrange taxi services for their guests, or you can hail a cab from the street or a designated taxi stand.

No matter which transportation option you choose, exploring Cappadocia is sure to be an unforgettable journey filled with breathtaking scenery, ancient wonders, and unforgettable experiences. So pack your bags, lace up your hiking boots, and get ready to embark on an adventure of a lifetime in this enchanting land.

AIRPORTS AND AIRLINES

Nestled in the heart of Turkey, Cappadocia may seem like a remote and ancient land, but thanks to its growing popularity as a tourist destination, it's easier than ever to reach by air. Whether you're flying in from Istanbul or Ankara, there are several airports in the region that cater to travelers from near and far.

1. Nevşehir Kapadokya Airport (NAV):

Located just 30 kilometers from the heart of Cappadocia, Nevşehir Kapadokya Airport is the primary gateway to the region for domestic and international travelers alike. This modern airport offers regular flights to and from Istanbul, Ankara, and other major cities in Turkey, as well as seasonal flights to select international destinations. With its convenient location and modern facilities, Nevşehir Kapadokya Airport provides a hassle-free way to begin your Cappadocian adventure.

2. Kayseri Erkilet Airport (ASR):

Situated approximately 70 kilometers from Cappadocia, Kayseri Erkilet Airport is another popular option for travelers flying into the region. This bustling airport offers a wide range of domestic and international flights, with regular service to and from Istanbul, Ankara, and other major cities in Turkey. While Kayseri Erkilet Airport is a bit farther from Cappadocia than Nevşehir Kapadokya Airport, it still provides convenient access to the region and is well-equipped to handle the needs of modern travelers.

3. Airlines Serving Cappadocia:

Several airlines offer flights to and from Cappadocia, providing travelers with a variety of options when it comes to planning their journey. Turkish Airlines, the national flag carrier of Turkey, operates regular flights to both Nevşehir Kapadokya Airport and Kayseri Erkilet Airport from its hub in Istanbul, making it a popular choice for travelers connecting from international destinations. Other airlines, such as Pegasus Airlines, AnadoluJet, and SunExpress, also offer regular service to Cappadocia from major cities in Turkey, providing travelers with plenty of flexibility when it comes to choosing their route.

4. Airport Facilities and Services:

Both Nevşehir Kapadokya Airport and Kayseri Erkilet Airport offer a range of facilities and services to ensure a comfortable and convenient travel experience. From car rental agencies and taxi services to cafes and souvenir shops, these airports are equipped to meet the needs of modern travelers. Additionally, many hotels and guesthouses in Cappadocia offer shuttle services to and from the airports, making it easy to reach your final destination with ease.

5. Tips for Flying to Cappadocia:

When flying to Cappadocia, it's important to book your tickets in advance, especially during peak travel seasons such as spring and fall. Additionally, be sure to check the baggage allowance and any visa requirements for your flight, and arrive at the airport with plenty of time to spare before your departure. With a little planning and preparation, flying to Cappadocia is a breeze, allowing you to focus on the excitement and adventure that awaits in this magical land.

Bus and Train Services

While Cappadocia's ancient charm may evoke visions of caravans traversing rocky terrain, modern travelers have a range of convenient transportation options at their disposal. From scenic bus rides through picturesque landscapes to the romance of train travel, getting around Cappadocia has never been easier.

1. Bus Services:

Bus travel is one of the most popular and convenient ways to explore Cappadocia, thanks to the region's well-developed network of bus routes and modern fleet of vehicles. Several bus companies operate services connecting major towns and attractions throughout Cappadocia, making it easy to travel between destinations. From Göreme to Uçhisar, Ürgüp to Avanos, buses run regularly throughout the day, providing travelers with a convenient and affordable way to get around.

2. Dolmuş (Shared Taxis):

For shorter journeys and trips to nearby villages, dolmuş, or shared taxis, are a popular choice among locals and travelers alike. These minibuses operate on fixed routes and can be hailed from designated stops along the roadside. With their frequent service and low fares, dolmuş offer a convenient and flexible way to explore Cappadocia's hidden gems without breaking the bank.

3. Train Services:

While train travel is not as common in Cappadocia as it is in other parts of Turkey, there are still options for those who prefer to travel by rail. The closest train station to Cappadocia is in Kayseri, approximately 70 kilometers away, which is served by regular trains from major cities such as Ankara and Istanbul. From Kayseri, travelers can take a taxi or bus to reach Cappadocia, making it a viable option for those looking to incorporate train travel into their journey.

4. Night Buses:

For travelers looking to maximize their time in Cappadocia and minimize travel expenses, night buses are a convenient option. Several bus companies operate overnight services from major cities such as Istanbul and Ankara, allowing travelers to sleep comfortably during the journey and wake up refreshed and ready to explore Cappadocia upon arrival. With reclining seats, onboard amenities, and affordable fares, night buses offer a convenient and hassle-free way to travel to and from Cappadocia.

5. Tips for Bus and Train Travel:

When traveling by bus or train in Cappadocia, it's important to book your tickets in advance, especially during peak travel seasons such as spring and fall. Additionally, be sure to arrive at the station early to ensure a smooth boarding process and avoid missing your departure. Lastly, don't forget to bring along snacks, water, and entertainment for the journey, as some routes may be long and lack onboard amenities.

Whether you're exploring the fairy chimneys of Göreme, wandering through the ancient streets of Ürgüp, or embarking on a scenic bus ride through the valleys of Cappadocia, bus and train services offer a convenient and affordable way to discover the region's many wonders. So sit back, relax, and enjoy the journey as you embark on an adventure of a lifetime in this enchanting land.

LOCAL PHRASES & LANGUAGE GUIDE

As you embark on your journey through the enchanting landscapes of Cappadocia, embracing the local language and customs can enrich your experience and deepen your connection to the region's rich heritage. While English is widely spoken in tourist areas, learning a few basic Turkish phrases can go a long way in fostering meaningful interactions and showing respect for the local culture.

1. Greetings:

Merhaba (MEHR-hah-bah) - Hello

Nasılsınız? (NAH-suhl-suhn-uhz) - How are you?

İyi günler (ee-YEE GOON-lehr) - Good day

Hoş geldiniz (hosh GEHL-dee-niz) - Welcome

2. Courtesy Phrases:

Teşekkür ederim (teh-shehk-KEWR eh-dehr-eem) - Thank you

Lütfen (LEWT-fehn) - Please

Özür dilerim (eu-ZUR dee-lehr-eem) - I'm sorry

Affedersiniz (ah-FEHD-ehr-see-niz) - Excuse me

3. Basic Conversational Phrases:

Evet (EH-veht) - Yes

Hayır (hah-YUHR) - No

Benim adım ___ (beh-NEEM ah-DEEM) - My name is ___

Ne kadar? (neh KAH-dahr) - How much?

4. Ordering Food and Drinks:

Bir ___ lütfen (beer _ lewt-fehn) - One ___ please

Menüyü görebilir miyim? (meh-NOO-yew geh-reh-bee-LEER mee-YEEM) - Can I see the menu?

Şu lütfen (shoo lewt-fehn) - Water please

İyi yemekler (ee-YEE yeh-MECK-lehr) - Enjoy your meal

5. Asking for Directions:

Nerede ___? (neh-REH-deh ___) - Where is ___?

Sağa (SAH-gah) - To the right

Sola (SOH-lah) - To the left

Düz (dooz) - Straight ahead

6. Emergency Phrases:

Yardım edin! (YAR-duhm eh-deen) - Help!

İmdat! (IM-daht) - Emergency!

Acil durum (ah-JEEL doo-ROOM) - Emergency

7. Expressing Gratitude:

Çok teşekkür ederim (chohk teh-shehk-KEWR eh-dehr-eem) - Thank you very much

Sizin yardımınız için teşekkür ederim (see-zeen yahr-duh-muh-NUZ ee-chin teh-shehk-KEWR eh-dehr-eem) - Thank you for your help

By incorporating these phrases into your conversations and interactions with locals, you'll not only navigate the region with greater ease but also show respect for the culture and traditions of Cappadocia. So don't be afraid to practice your Turkish, engage with the locals, and immerse yourself in the vibrant tapestry of language and life that awaits you in this magical land. Hoş geldiniz (Welcome) to Cappadocia!

Where to Stay in Cappadocia

ACCOMMODATION OPTIONS

Nestled amidst the captivating landscapes of Cappadocia are a plethora of accommodation options, each offering a unique blend of comfort, charm, and hospitality. Whether you're seeking the rustic allure of a cave hotel or the modern amenities of a boutique inn, there's something to suit every taste and budget in this enchanting region.

1. Cave Hotels:

One of the most iconic and beloved accommodation options in Cappadocia is the cave hotel. Carved into the soft tufa rock that defines the region's landscape, these unique hotels offer guests the chance to experience life in a traditional cave dwelling while enjoying modern comforts and amenities. From cozy alcoves and stone archways to panoramic terraces with breathtaking views, staying in a cave hotel is a truly unforgettable experience that captures the spirit of Cappadocia's ancient heritage.

2. Boutique Hotels and Guesthouses:

For travelers seeking a more contemporary and luxurious experience, boutique hotels and guesthouses abound in Cappadocia. These charming establishments offer stylish accommodations, personalized service, and a range of amenities such as spa facilities, gourmet restaurants, and rooftop lounges. Whether you're unwinding in a jacuzzi suite with panoramic views of the fairy chimneys or savoring a gourmet breakfast on a sun-drenched terrace, boutique hotels and guesthouses provide an indulgent retreat in the heart of Cappadocia.

3. Budget Accommodation:

Travelers on a budget need not worry about finding affordable accommodations in Cappadocia. From cozy hostels and guesthouses to budget-friendly hotels and pensions, there are plenty of options available for those looking to stretch their lira without sacrificing comfort or convenience. Many budget accommodations offer clean and comfortable rooms, complimentary breakfast, and friendly service, making them an ideal choice for budget-conscious travelers seeking a memorable stay in Cappadocia.

4. Luxury Resorts:

For those seeking the ultimate in luxury and indulgence, Cappadocia boasts a selection of world-class resorts and spa retreats. Set amidst lush gardens, vineyards, and panoramic vistas, these lavish properties offer opulent accommodations, exquisite dining experiences, and an array of amenities such as infinity pools, wellness centers, and private hot air balloon rides. Whether you're lounging in a sumptuous suite with a fireplace and jacuzzi or indulging in a traditional Turkish hammam, luxury resorts in Cappadocia provide a lavish escape for discerning travelers.

5. Unique Stays:

In addition to traditional hotels and resorts, Cappadocia also offers a range of unique and offbeat accommodation options for adventurous travelers. From glamping under the stars in a luxury tent to sleeping in a restored cave monastery or ancient Greek mansion, there's no shortage of quirky and memorable places to stay in this enchanting region. Whether you're seeking an immersive cultural experience or simply want to sleep somewhere out of the ordinary, Cappadocia's unique stays offer a one-of-a-kind adventure that you'll remember for years to come.

No matter which accommodation option you choose, you're sure to find a warm welcome and a comfortable home away from home in the captivating landscapes of Cappadocia. So pack your bags, choose your lodgings, and get ready for an unforgettable stay in this magical land.

CAVE HOTELS AND BOUTIQUE STAYS

Nestled within the ancient rock formations of Cappadocia lie some of the world's most enchanting accommodations: cave hotels and boutique stays. Carved into the soft tufa rock that defines the region's landscape, these unique lodgings offer guests an immersive experience unlike any other, blending modern luxury with the timeless allure of Cappadocia's ancient heritage.

1. Cave Hotels:

Stepping into a cave hotel in Cappadocia is like stepping back in time to a world of ancient wonders and hidden treasures. These remarkable accommodations, carved into the rock by generations of inhabitants, offer guests the chance to sleep in a space that has been shaped by centuries of history and tradition. From cozy alcoves and winding passageways to soaring ceilings and panoramic vistas, each cave hotel is a testament to the ingenuity and craftsmanship of its creators.

Guests can expect to find all the modern amenities they desire, including plush bedding, spacious bathrooms, and in-room heating and cooling, all seamlessly integrated into the natural rock surroundings. Many cave hotels also feature charming touches such as hand-carved furniture, local artwork, and traditional Turkish rugs, creating a warm and inviting atmosphere that feels like home.

But perhaps the most magical aspect of staying in a cave hotel is the opportunity to immerse oneself in the tranquility and beauty of Cappadocia's rugged landscape. Whether enjoying breakfast on a sun-drenched terrace overlooking the fairy chimneys or sipping wine by a crackling fire in a cozy cave alcove, guests can't help but be captivated by the breathtaking views and timeless charm of their surroundings.

2. Boutique Stays:

For travelers seeking a more contemporary and intimate experience, boutique stays in Cappadocia offer a perfect blend of style, comfort, and personalized service. These charming accommodations, often housed in historic buildings or restored cave dwellings, provide guests with a boutique hotel experience that is both luxurious and authentic.

Each boutique stay is uniquely designed to reflect the character and heritage of its surroundings, with stylish furnishings, modern amenities, and thoughtful touches that create a warm and welcoming atmosphere. Whether you're unwinding in a jacuzzi suite with panoramic views of the valley or savoring a gourmet meal prepared with locally sourced ingredients, boutique stays in Cappadocia offer an indulgent retreat for discerning travelers.

But beyond the creature comforts, what truly sets boutique stays apart is the personalized service and attention to detail that guests receive. From arranging private tours and hot air balloon rides to recommending hidden gems and local eateries, the staff at boutique stays go above and beyond to ensure that every aspect of your stay is unforgettable.

In the end, whether you choose to spend your nights in a centuries-old cave hotel or a stylish boutique stay, one thing is certain: your experience in Cappadocia will be nothing short of magical. So pack your bags, embrace the mystique, and get ready for an unforgettable adventure in this captivating land of fairy chimneys and ancient wonders.

BUDGET, MID-RANGE, AND LUXURY OPTIONS

As you embark on your journey to the captivating landscapes of Cappadocia, you'll find a wide array of accommodation options to suit every budget and preference. Whether you're seeking a cozy cave retreat, a stylish boutique hotel, or a luxurious resort experience, Cappadocia offers something for every traveler, from budget-conscious backpackers to discerning luxury seekers.

1. Budget Options:

For travelers seeking comfortable and affordable accommodations without breaking the bank, Cappadocia offers a range of budget-friendly options. Cozy guesthouses, family-run pensions, and backpacker hostels abound in towns like Göreme, Ürgüp, and Avanos, providing clean and comfortable rooms at wallet-friendly prices. These budget accommodations often include amenities such as complimentary breakfast, free Wi-Fi, and friendly staff who are happy to offer tips and recommendations for exploring the local area.

Additionally, camping is a popular option for adventurous travelers looking to immerse themselves in Cappadocia's stunning natural beauty. Several campsites and outdoor adventure companies offer tent rentals and organized camping trips, allowing travelers to sleep under the stars amidst the region's breathtaking landscapes.

2. Mid-range Options:

For travelers seeking a balance of comfort and value, Cappadocia offers a variety of mid-range accommodation options that provide a higher level of comfort and amenities without breaking the bank. From charming boutique hotels and guesthouses to traditional cave dwellings and restored Ottoman mansions, mid-range accommodations in Cappadocia offer a blend of modern convenience and local charm.

Guests can expect to find spacious rooms, stylish furnishings, and a range of amenities such as on-site restaurants, swimming pools, and wellness facilities. Many mid-range accommodations also offer personalized service and special touches to make guests feel welcome, such as complimentary welcome drinks, guided tours, and cultural experiences.

3. Luxury Options:

For travelers seeking the ultimate in comfort, luxury, and indulgence, Cappadocia offers a selection of world-class resorts, boutique hotels, and spa retreats that cater to every whim and desire. Set amidst lush gardens, vineyards, and panoramic vistas, these lavish properties provide guests with an unforgettable experience of opulence and relaxation.

Luxury accommodations in Cappadocia boast spacious suites and villas, lavish furnishings, and a range of amenities such as private terraces, infinity pools, and gourmet dining options. Guests can indulge in pampering spa treatments, take part in exclusive experiences such as private hot air balloon rides and wine tastings, and enjoy impeccable service from attentive staff who anticipate their every need.

Whether you're traveling on a shoestring budget, seeking a comfortable mid-range retreat, or indulging in a luxurious escape, Cappadocia offers accommodation options to suit every traveler's taste and budget. So pack your bags, choose your lodgings, and get ready to embark on an unforgettable journey through this magical land of fairy chimneys and ancient wonders.

LOCAL INSIGHTS: RECOMMENDATIONS FROM LOCALS ON HIDDEN GEMS FOR ACCOMMODATION

While the fairy chimneys and ancient cave dwellings of Cappadocia are well-known around the world, the region is also home to a wealth of hidden gems when it comes to accommodation options. From secluded cave hotels nestled in remote valleys to charming guesthouses tucked away in historic villages, locals in Cappadocia have a treasure trove of recommendations for those seeking a truly authentic and unforgettable stay.

1. Ali's Cave Retreat:

Tucked away in a tranquil valley just outside of Göreme, Ali's Cave Retreat is a hidden gem beloved by locals and travelers alike. Run by Ali and his family, this cozy cave hotel offers guests a chance to experience life in a traditional Cappadocian cave dwelling while enjoying modern comforts and personalized service. With just a handful of rooms carved into the rock, guests can enjoy peace and privacy amidst breathtaking natural scenery, with Ali always on hand to share his insider tips and recommendations for exploring the local area.

2. Ayşe's Vineyard House:

For travelers seeking a true taste of Cappadocian hospitality, Ayşe's Vineyard House is the perfect choice. Located in the picturesque village of Uçhisar, this charming guesthouse offers cozy accommodations in a restored Ottoman mansion surrounded by vineyards and orchards. Guests can enjoy leisurely breakfasts on the terrace overlooking the valley, explore the nearby hiking trails and ancient ruins, and sample Ayşe's homemade jams and wines made from the grapes grown on the property.

3. Mehmet's Cave Monastery:

Nestled in a secluded valley on the outskirts of Ürgüp, Mehmet's Cave Monastery offers a truly unique and immersive accommodation experience. Housed in a restored Byzantine-era monastery carved into the rock, this intimate retreat offers guests a chance to step back in time and experience the region's rich history and culture up close. With just a handful of rooms and a serene courtyard garden, guests can enjoy peace and tranquility amidst stunning natural surroundings, with Mehmet always on hand to share his knowledge and passion for Cappadocia's ancient heritage.

4. Fatma's Traditional Mansion:

In the heart of Avanos, Fatma's Traditional Mansion offers guests a chance to experience life in a beautifully restored Ottoman-era mansion. With its elegant architecture, spacious rooms, and lush courtyard garden, this boutique hotel provides a peaceful oasis in the midst of the bustling town. Guests can explore the nearby pottery workshops and historic landmarks, relax with a cup of çay in the traditional Turkish salon, and savor homemade meals prepared with love by Fatma herself.

5. Hasan's Hilltop Retreat:

Perched on a hilltop overlooking the village of Ortahisar, Hasan's Hilltop Retreat offers panoramic views of the surrounding valleys and fairy chimneys. This rustic yet charming guesthouse provides guests with cozy accommodations in traditional stone cottages, each with its own private terrace or balcony. Guests can unwind by the fireplace in the communal lounge, take leisurely walks through the orchards and vineyards, and enjoy authentic Turkish hospitality from Hasan and his family.

These are just a few of the hidden gems recommended by locals in Cappadocia, each offering a unique and unforgettable accommodation experience that captures the spirit of this magical land. Whether you're seeking a cozy cave retreat, a charming village guesthouse, or a secluded hilltop sanctuary, Cappadocia has something for every traveler's taste and preference. So why not venture off the beaten path and discover your own hidden gem in this enchanting region?

Exploring Cappadocia's Highlights

GOREME OPEN-AIR MUSEUM

Nestled within the otherworldly landscapes of Cappadocia lies a place of profound spiritual significance and historical richness: the Göreme Open-Air Museum. This UNESCO World Heritage Site is a testament to the region's rich cultural heritage and the enduring legacy of its early Christian inhabitants, whose cave churches and monastic complexes date back over a millennium.

Exploring the Ancient Churches:

At the heart of the Göreme Open-Air Museum are its remarkable rock-cut churches, each adorned with vibrant frescoes that offer a glimpse into the religious and artistic traditions of Cappadocia's past. Visitors can wander through the labyrinthine corridors and cavernous chambers of these ancient churches, marveling at the intricate designs and vivid colors that adorn their walls and ceilings. From the richly decorated interiors of the Dark Church to the serene simplicity of the Apple Church, each chapel offers a unique and immersive experience that transports visitors back in time to a world of faith and devotion.

Discovering Monastic Life:

In addition to its churches, the Göreme Open-Air Museum is home to a series of monastic complexes that provide insights into the daily lives of Cappadocia's early Christian communities. Visitors can explore the monk cells, communal kitchens, and refectories that once housed the monks who called this place home, gaining a deeper understanding of the ascetic lifestyle and spiritual practices that were central to their way of life. From the towering cliffs of the Üzümlü Church to the secluded courtyards of the Tokalı Church, each monastery offers a glimpse into a world of solitude, contemplation, and prayer.

Preserving Cultural Heritage:

The Göreme Open-Air Museum serves not only as a showcase of Cappadocia's cultural heritage but also as a testament to the ongoing efforts to preserve and protect this unique site for future generations. Through careful conservation and restoration efforts, the rock-cut churches and monastic complexes of Göreme have been painstakingly preserved, ensuring that visitors can continue to experience the beauty and wonder of this ancient site for years to come. Moreover, the museum's informative exhibits and guided tours provide valuable insights into the history, art, and architecture of Cappadocia, fostering a deeper appreciation for the region's rich cultural legacy.

Embracing Spiritual Significance:

For many visitors, a visit to the Göreme Open-Air Museum is not merely a journey through history but also a spiritual pilgrimage—a chance to connect with the sacred and the divine in a place of profound significance. Whether marveling at the intricacies of Byzantine art, contemplating the solitude of the monk's cell, or simply soaking in the serene beauty of the surrounding landscape, visitors to the Göreme Open-Air Museum are invited to embark on a journey of discovery, reflection, and renewal—an experience that transcends time and space and speaks to the soul.

In the end, the Göreme Open-Air Museum stands as a testament to the enduring legacy of Cappadocia's early Christian communities and the timeless beauty of its rock-cut architecture. As visitors wander through its ancient churches and monastic complexes, they are invited to uncover the secrets of the past, explore the depths of the human spirit, and immerse themselves in the rich cultural tapestry of this enchanting region.

FAIRY CHIMNEYS OF PASABAG VALLEY

Nestled within the captivating landscapes of Cappadocia lies a natural wonder that seems straight out of a fairytale: the Fairy Chimneys of Pasabag Valley. This surreal landscape, characterized by its towering rock formations and whimsical shapes, is a testament to the region's geological wonders and the fascinating processes that have shaped its unique terrain over millions of years.

1. Geological Marvels:

The Fairy Chimneys of Pasabag Valley, also known as Monks Valley, are the result of millions of years of geological activity and erosion. These towering rock formations, which resemble giant mushrooms or otherworldly spires, were formed through the gradual erosion of volcanic ash and lava deposits, sculpted by the elements into their distinctive shapes over millennia. Today, they stand as silent sentinels, bearing witness to the forces of nature and the passage of time.

2. Historical Significance:

In addition to their natural beauty, the Fairy Chimneys of Pasabag Valley hold great historical and cultural significance. The valley was once home to a thriving monastic community, who sought refuge in the secluded caves and rock-cut dwellings that dot the landscape. These early Christian monks, known as the "stony ascetics," lived a life of solitude and prayer amidst the otherworldly beauty of the valley, leaving behind a rich legacy of spirituality and devotion that still resonates today.

3. Whimsical Atmosphere:

Wandering through the Fairy Chimneys of Pasabag Valley is like stepping into a dream—a world of surreal shapes and enchanting vistas that captivate the imagination and stir the soul. Visitors can explore the winding pathways and hidden alcoves of the valley, marveling at the towering chimneys and intricate rock formations that loom overhead. Whether basking in the golden light of sunrise or watching the colors of sunset dance across the sky, the Fairy Chimneys of Pasabag Valley offer a magical backdrop for unforgettable moments and timeless memories.

4. Cultural Insights:

The Fairy Chimneys of Pasabag Valley are not only a natural wonder but also a cultural treasure, offering insights into the history, art, and traditions of Cappadocia's past. Visitors can learn about the region's rich heritage through informative signs and guided tours, discovering the stories of the monks who once inhabited the valley and the ancient civilizations that called this land home. Moreover, the valley is a popular spot for local artists and artisans, who draw inspiration from its otherworldly beauty to create works of art that reflect the spirit of Cappadocia.

5. Spiritual Retreat:

For many visitors, the Fairy Chimneys of Pasabag Valley offer more than just a scenic attraction—they provide a sanctuary for contemplation, reflection, and spiritual renewal. Whether sitting quietly amidst the towering chimneys or embarking on a meditative walk through the valley, visitors are invited to connect with the natural world and the deeper mysteries of existence. In this tranquil landscape, surrounded by the timeless beauty of nature, it's easy to feel a sense of awe and wonder that transcends words and touches the soul.

In the end, the Fairy Chimneys of Pasabag Valley are more than just a geological oddity—they are a symbol of the enduring beauty and mystery of Cappadocia, a place where nature, history, and spirituality converge in a harmonious dance. Whether exploring their whimsical shapes, pondering their ancient origins, or simply basking in their ethereal beauty, visitors to Pasabag Valley are sure to be enchanted by this magical corner of the world.

HOT AIR BALLOON RIDES

One of the most iconic experiences in Cappadocia is taking to the skies in a hot air balloon—a breathtaking adventure that offers unparalleled views of the region's stunning landscapes and ancient wonders. From the fairy chimneys and rock formations to the valleys and historic villages below, a hot air balloon ride is a once-in-a-lifetime opportunity to see Cappadocia from a whole new perspective.

1. A Surreal Sunrise Experience:

As the sun begins to rise over the horizon, casting its golden glow across the rugged terrain of Cappadocia, hot air balloons begin to take flight, painting the sky with a kaleidoscope of colors. There's nothing quite like the sensation of floating effortlessly above the earth, with the gentle hum of the balloon's burner and the crisp morning air filling your senses. As you ascend higher and higher into the sky, the landscapes of Cappadocia unfold beneath you in all their glory, revealing a world of breathtaking beauty and timeless wonder.

2. Unforgettable Views:

From the vantage point of a hot air balloon, the landscapes of Cappadocia take on a whole new dimension, revealing hidden valleys, ancient rock formations, and historic landmarks that are inaccessible by any other means. As you drift silently through the sky, you'll have the opportunity to marvel at the surreal shapes of the fairy chimneys, the rugged beauty of the valleys, and the intricate patterns of the ancient cave dwellings that dot the landscape. With 360-degree views stretching as far as the eye can see, a hot air balloon ride offers an unparalleled perspective on the natural and cultural wonders of Cappadocia.

3. A Sense of Serenity and Freedom:

There's something inherently peaceful and serene about drifting through the sky in a hot air balloon, with nothing but the wind and the sound of your own breath to accompany you on your journey. As you glide silently above the earth, you'll feel a sense of freedom and liberation unlike anything you've ever experienced before. With no set itinerary or destination, each hot air balloon ride is a unique and spontaneous adventure, guided only by the whims of the wind and the skill of your pilot.

4. An Experience of a Lifetime:

For many travelers, a hot air balloon ride in Cappadocia is the highlight of their trip—a bucket-list experience that leaves a lasting impression and creates memories that will be cherished for a lifetime. Whether you're celebrating a special occasion, embarking on a romantic getaway, or simply seeking a thrilling adventure, a hot air balloon ride offers an unforgettable experience that captures the spirit of Cappadocia in all its beauty and wonder.

5. Practical Considerations:

Before booking a hot air balloon ride in Cappadocia, it's important to consider a few practicalities. Balloon rides are typically conducted in the early morning hours, when weather conditions are most favorable, so be prepared to wake up before dawn to catch the sunrise. It's also a good idea to dress warmly and wear comfortable clothing, as temperatures can be quite cool at high altitudes. Lastly, be sure to book your balloon ride in advance, especially during peak travel seasons, as they tend to fill up quickly.

In the end, a hot air balloon ride in Cappadocia is more than just a journey through the sky—it's a magical adventure that allows you to see the world with fresh eyes and experience the beauty of nature in all its splendor. So why not take to the skies and embark on an unforgettable aerial odyssey above the enchanting landscapes of Cappadocia?

LOVE VALLEY AND ROSE VALLEY

Nestled within the captivating landscapes of Cappadocia are two enchanting destinations that beckon travelers with their natural beauty and serene ambiance: Love Valley and Rose Valley. These two valleys, known for their striking rock formations, lush vegetation, and breathtaking vistas, offer visitors a chance to immerse themselves in the tranquility and splendor of Cappadocia's wilderness.

1. Love Valley:

As the name suggests, Love Valley is a place of romance and enchantment—a landscape sculpted by the forces of nature into surreal shapes and formations that evoke the imagination and stir the soul. The valley is characterized by its towering rock formations, known as "fairy chimneys," which rise majestically from the earth like ancient sentinels guarding the secrets of the land. These unique formations, with their phallic-like appearance, have earned Love Valley its reputation as a symbol of fertility and love, making it a popular destination for couples and honeymooners seeking a romantic escape.

2. Rose Valley:

Adjacent to Love Valley lies Rose Valley, named for the rosy hues that bathe its rugged cliffs and rock formations in the soft light of dawn and dusk. This picturesque valley is renowned for its breathtaking scenery, with winding trails that meander through lush vineyards, orchards, and wildflower meadows. Visitors can explore the valley on foot or by bike, following ancient pathways that lead to hidden caves, rock-cut churches, and panoramic viewpoints that offer sweeping vistas of the surrounding landscapes. With its tranquil ambiance and natural splendor, Rose Valley is a paradise for nature lovers and outdoor enthusiasts alike.

3. Hiking and Exploration:

Both Love Valley and Rose Valley offer ample opportunities for hiking and exploration, with a network of well-marked trails that wind through their rugged terrain. Whether you're embarking on a leisurely stroll through the valley floor or tackling a more challenging hike to one of the higher viewpoints, you'll be rewarded with stunning scenery and unforgettable experiences at every turn. Along the way, keep an eye out for the ancient rock-cut churches and hidden caves that dot the landscape, offering glimpses into the region's rich history and cultural heritage.

4. Sunset and Sunrise Views:

One of the highlights of visiting Love Valley and Rose Valley is experiencing the magical light of sunrise and sunset as it bathes the landscape in a golden glow. As the sun rises or sets over the horizon, the rocky cliffs and fairy chimneys of the valleys are transformed into a kaleidoscope of colors, creating a mesmerizing spectacle that is truly unforgettable. Whether you're capturing the moment on camera or simply basking in the beauty of nature, watching the sunrise or sunset in Love Valley and Rose Valley is an experience that will stay with you long after you've left Cappadocia behind.

In the end, Love Valley and Rose Valley are more than just geological wonders—they're sanctuaries of natural beauty and tranquility that invite visitors to slow down, reconnect with the earth, and embrace the timeless rhythms of the natural world. So why not wander off the beaten path and discover the hidden treasures of Love Valley and Rose Valley on your next journey through Cappadocia

UÇHISAR CASTLE

Perched majestically atop the highest point in Cappadocia, Uçhisar Castle stands as a timeless sentinel, offering panoramic views of the surrounding valleys, fairy chimneys, and ancient villages. Carved into the towering rock formations that define the region's landscape, this ancient fortress has witnessed centuries of history and serves as a testament to the ingenuity and resilience of Cappadocia's inhabitants.

1. A Living Legacy:

Constructed by the Byzantines during the early medieval period and later expanded and fortified by the Seljuks and Ottomans, Uçhisar Castle has played a central role in the region's history for over a millennium. Originally built as a defensive stronghold to protect against invading forces, the castle's strategic location atop a steep hill provided its inhabitants with unparalleled views of the surrounding valleys and plains, allowing them to monitor and defend the region against potential threats.

2. Architectural Marvels:

The castle itself is a marvel of ancient architecture, with its labyrinthine corridors, winding staircases, and hidden chambers carved directly into the rock. Visitors can explore the castle's interior, marveling at the intricate carvings, vaulted ceilings, and ancient graffiti that adorn its walls. From the highest vantage points, they can gaze out over the breathtaking landscapes of Cappadocia, taking in sweeping vistas of fairy chimneys, vineyards, and historic villages that stretch as far as the eye can see.

3. Cultural Heritage:

In addition to its architectural significance, Uçhisar Castle is also a cultural treasure, offering insights into the history, art, and traditions of Cappadocia's past. Visitors can learn about the castle's rich history through informative exhibits and guided tours, discovering the stories of the rulers, warriors, and artisans who once inhabited its walls. Moreover, the castle's strategic location at the crossroads of ancient trade routes made it a melting pot of cultures and civilizations, influencing the region's art, architecture, and cuisine in profound ways.

4. Panoramic Views:

One of the highlights of visiting Uçhisar Castle is the opportunity to take in the breathtaking views from its highest points. Whether you're watching the sunrise over the horizon, witnessing the colors of sunset dance across the sky, or simply soaking in the beauty of the surrounding landscapes, the panoramic vistas from Uçhisar Castle are sure to leave you spellbound. With each passing moment, the ever-changing light and shadows cast new perspectives on the timeless beauty of

Cappadocia, creating an unforgettable experience for visitors of all ages.

5. A Symbol of Resilience:

As you explore the ancient corridors and towering battlements of Uçhisar Castle, you can't help but be struck by the sense of resilience and strength that emanates from its weathered walls. Despite centuries of upheaval and change, the castle has stood the test of time, serving as a symbol of endurance and perseverance in the face of adversity. Today, it stands as a reminder of the indomitable spirit of Cappadocia's people and the enduring legacy of its rich cultural heritage.

In the end, a visit to Uçhisar Castle is more than just a journey through history—it's an opportunity to connect with the ancient rhythms of Cappadocia, to immerse yourself in the timeless beauty of its landscapes, and to experience the magic of this enchanting region in all its glory. So why not step back in time and discover the wonders of Uçhisar Castle on your next adventure through Cappadocia?

LOCAL INSIGHTS: PHOTOGRAPHER'S PERSPECTIVE - PHOTOGRAPHY TIPS FOR CAPTURING CAPPADOCIA'S BEAUTY

As a photographer living amidst the enchanting landscapes of Cappadocia, I've had the privilege of witnessing the region's beauty in all its glory—and capturing it through the lens of my camera. From the surreal rock formations and ancient cave dwellings to the vibrant colors of sunrise and sunset, Cappadocia offers endless opportunities for photographers to create stunning images that capture the essence of this magical land. Here are some photography tips from a local perspective to help you make the most of your photographic journey through Cappadocia:

1. Embrace the Golden Hours:

One of the best times to photograph Cappadocia is during the golden hours—just after sunrise and before sunset—when the soft, golden light bathes the landscape in a warm, ethereal glow. During these times, the colors are richer, the shadows are softer, and the textures are more pronounced, creating the perfect conditions for capturing stunning photos. Be sure to wake up early and stay out late to make the most of these magical moments.

2. Explore Off-the-Beaten-Path Locations:

While iconic sites like Göreme and Uçhisar Castle are undoubtedly beautiful, some of the most captivating photographic opportunities in Cappadocia can be found off the beaten path. Take the time to explore lesser-known villages, hidden valleys, and remote viewpoints, where you'll find unique compositions and perspectives that are less crowded and more authentic. Don't be afraid to wander off the main tourist trails and discover the hidden gems that make Cappadocia truly special.

3. Experiment with Composition and Framing:

Cappadocia's landscapes are incredibly diverse and dynamic, offering photographers endless opportunities to experiment with composition and framing. Whether you're capturing the sweeping curves of the fairy chimneys, the intricate details of a rock-cut church, or the vastness of a panoramic vista, don't be afraid to get creative with your compositions. Play around with different angles, perspectives, and focal points to create images that are visually compelling and emotionally evocative.

4. Capture the Human Element:

While Cappadocia's natural landscapes are undeniably stunning, don't forget to include the human element in your photos as well. Whether it's a local farmer tending to his fields, a group of children playing in the streets, or a hot air balloon drifting gracefully through the sky, including people in your photos adds depth, context, and a sense of scale to your images. Be respectful and considerate when photographing locals, and always ask for permission before taking their picture.

5. Be Prepared for Changing Conditions:

Cappadocia's weather can be unpredictable, with sudden changes in light, weather, and atmospheric conditions. Be prepared to adapt to changing conditions on the fly, whether it's adjusting your camera settings, changing your composition, or waiting patiently for the perfect moment to capture the shot. Bring along a tripod for stability, a variety of lenses for different perspectives, and plenty of spare batteries and memory cards to ensure you don't miss any opportunities.

6. Respect the Environment and Culture:

Above all, remember to respect the environment and culture of Cappadocia as you explore and photograph the region. Stay on designated trails, refrain from climbing or disturbing delicate rock formations, and always ask for permission before photographing people or private property. By being mindful and respectful of your surroundings, you'll not only create better photographs but also help preserve the natural beauty and cultural heritage of Cappadocia for future generations to enjoy.

In the end, capturing the beauty of Cappadocia through photography is as much about immersing yourself in the moment as it is about technical skill and equipment. So slow down, take a deep breath, and allow yourself to be fully present as you explore this magical land with your camera in hand. With a little patience, creativity, and respect, you'll create images that not only capture the essence of Cappadocia but also inspire others to see the world in a new light.

Outdoor Activities in Cappadocia

HIKING AND TREKKING TRAILS

Nestled amidst the otherworldly landscapes of Cappadocia are a network of hiking and trekking trails that offer adventurers the opportunity to explore the region's natural beauty, ancient wonders, and hidden treasures on foot. Whether you're a seasoned hiker seeking a challenge or a casual explorer looking for a leisurely stroll, Cappadocia has trails to suit every skill level and interest.

1. Rose Valley and Red Valley:

One of the most popular hiking destinations in Cappadocia is the Rose Valley and Red Valley trail, which winds its way through a picturesque landscape of rose-colored cliffs, lush vineyards, and ancient rock-cut churches. Along the way, hikers can explore hidden caves, panoramic viewpoints, and historic landmarks, including the famous Çavuşin Church and the iconic Three Sisters rock formation. With its gentle terrain and breathtaking scenery, this trail is perfect for hikers of all ages and abilities.

2. Pigeon Valley:

For a leisurely stroll with stunning views, head to Pigeon Valley—a scenic trail that follows the path of an ancient riverbed lined with towering cliffs and cave dwellings. Named for the thousands of pigeon houses carved into the rock by early inhabitants, Pigeon Valley offers hikers the chance to immerse themselves in Cappadocia's rich history and natural beauty. Along the way, keep an eye out for the resident wildlife, including colorful birds and elusive foxes, that call the valley home.

3. Ihlara Valley:

For a more challenging trek, venture to the Ihlara Valley—a verdant gorge carved by the meandering waters of the Melendiz River. This spectacular trail takes hikers past towering cliffs, lush vegetation, and ancient rock-cut churches, including the impressive Ağaçaltı Church and the imposing Selime Monastery. With its rugged terrain and steep ascents, the Ihlara Valley trail is best suited for experienced hikers looking for a full-day adventure.

4. Güvercinlik Valley (Pigeon Valley) to Göreme:

For those looking to combine hiking with sightseeing, the trail from Güvercinlik Valley to Göreme offers the perfect blend of natural beauty and cultural heritage. This scenic route winds its way through the picturesque valleys and fairy chimneys of Cappadocia, passing by ancient rock formations, historic villages, and iconic landmarks such as Uçhisar Castle and Göreme Open-Air Museum. Whether you're hiking solo or joining a guided tour, this trail provides an unforgettable journey through the heart of Cappadocia.

5. Practical Considerations:

Before setting out on any hiking or trekking adventure in Cappadocia, it's important to take some practical considerations into account. Be sure to wear sturdy hiking shoes, dress in layers to accommodate changing weather conditions, and carry plenty of water and snacks to stay hydrated and energized along the way. Additionally, always stay on designated trails, respect local wildlife and vegetation, and be mindful of any cultural or historical sites you encounter during your hike.

In the end, exploring Cappadocia's hiking and trekking trails is not just about the destination—it's about the journey itself, and the unforgettable experiences and memories you'll create along the way. So lace up your boots, pack your sense of adventure, and get ready to embark on an epic hiking adventure through the stunning landscapes of Cappadocia.

CYCLING ROUTES

Cappadocia's captivating landscapes and ancient wonders make it a cyclist's dream destination. With its network of scenic routes winding through fairy-tale valleys, historic villages, and surreal rock formations, Cappadocia offers cyclists of all levels an unforgettable journey through one of Turkey's most enchanting regions.

1. Göreme to Uçhisar:

One of the most popular cycling routes in Cappadocia is the scenic journey from Göreme to Uçhisar—a picturesque route that takes cyclists past some of the region's most iconic landmarks. Starting in Göreme, cyclists can pedal through the stunning landscapes of Love Valley and Pigeon Valley, with their towering fairy chimneys and ancient cave dwellings providing a dramatic backdrop for the ride. As cyclists approach Uçhisar, they'll be treated to panoramic views of the iconic

Uçhisar Castle, perched high atop a towering rock formation, making for a truly unforgettable cycling experience.

2. Ürgüp to Ortahisar:

For those seeking a more leisurely ride, the cycling route from Ürgüp to Ortahisar offers a scenic journey through some of Cappadocia's most charming villages and valleys. Starting in Ürgüp, cyclists can pedal through the rolling vineyards and orchards of the region, stopping to sample local wines and traditional cuisine along the way. As they make their way towards Ortahisar, cyclists will pass through the picturesque valleys of Red Valley and Rose Valley, with their striking rock formations and ancient cave churches providing plenty of opportunities for exploration and photography.

3. Avanos to Çavuşin:

For a more adventurous cycling experience, the route from Avanos to Çavuşin offers cyclists the chance to explore some of Cappadocia's lesser-known gems. Starting in the historic town of Avanos, cyclists can pedal through the lush landscapes of Zelve Valley, with its ancient cave dwellings and dramatic rock formations. As they continue on towards Çavuşin, cyclists will pass through the charming villages of Cavusin and Pasabag, with their traditional stone houses and historic churches providing a glimpse into the region's rich history and culture.

4. Practical Tips:

Before setting out on any cycling adventure in Cappadocia, it's important to come prepared. Be sure to wear comfortable clothing and sturdy shoes, and carry plenty of water, snacks, and sun protection. Additionally, always stay on designated cycling routes and be mindful of local traffic and road conditions. For those looking to explore off the beaten path, guided cycling tours are available, offering expert guidance and insight into the region's history, culture, and natural beauty.

In the end, cycling in Cappadocia is not just about the physical journey—it's about immersing yourself in the region's rich history, culture, and natural beauty, and experiencing the magic of this enchanting destination from a unique perspective. So saddle up, grab your helmet, and get ready to pedal your way through paradise on an unforgettable cycling adventure in Cappadocia.

LOCAL INSIGHTS: ADVENTURE STORIES AND RECOMMENDED OUTDOOR EXPERIENCES BY LOCALS

Cappadocia isn't just a place; it's a living, breathing adventure waiting to be explored. And who better to guide you through its secret treasures and thrilling experiences than the locals themselves? Here are some adventure stories and recommended outdoor experiences straight from the hearts of those who call Cappadocia home.

1. Hot Air Ballooning:

"Imagine drifting silently above the surreal landscapes of Cappadocia as the first rays of sunlight paint the sky in shades of gold and pink. That's the magic of hot air ballooning in Cappadocia—an experience that never fails to take your breath away.

From the thrill of lift-off to the serenity of floating above ancient valleys and fairy chimneys, hot air ballooning offers a perspective on Cappadocia's beauty that you simply can't get anywhere else." - Mehmet, Hot Air Balloon Pilot

2. Rock Climbing in Ihlara Valley:

"For adrenaline junkies like me, there's nothing quite like the thrill of rock climbing in Ihlara Valley. With its towering cliffs, challenging routes, and breathtaking views, the valley offers endless opportunities for adventure and exploration. Whether you're a beginner or an experienced climber, there's something for everyone here, from easy bouldering spots to multi-pitch routes that will test your skills and push your limits." - Ayşe, Rock Climbing Enthusiast

3. Horseback Riding in Love Valley:

"As a local equestrian, I can tell you there's no better way to experience the beauty of Cappadocia than on horseback. Riding through Love Valley, with its surreal rock formations and panoramic vistas, feels like stepping back in time to a land of fairy tales and legends. Whether you're a seasoned rider or a novice, there are guided horseback tours available for all skill levels, allowing you to explore Cappadocia's hidden gems from a unique and unforgettable perspective." - Mustafa, Horseback Riding Guide

4. Cycling through Fairy Chimneys:

"Cycling through the winding trails and fairy chimneys of Cappadocia is a dream come true for outdoor enthusiasts like me. From gentle rides through picturesque valleys to challenging mountain biking trails that will test your skills, Cappadocia offers something for cyclists of all abilities. And with stunning views around every corner and plenty of quaint villages to explore along the way, it's an adventure you won't soon forget." - Deniz, Cycling Enthusiast

5. Exploring Underground Cities:

"As a local historian, I've spent countless hours exploring the ancient underground cities of Cappadocia, and each time, I'm filled with a sense of wonder and awe. From the intricate passageways and hidden chambers to the ingenious ventilation systems and underground churches, these cities are a testament to the ingenuity and resilience of Cappadocia's early inhabitants. For a truly immersive experience, I recommend joining a guided tour led by a knowledgeable local guide who can share the stories and secrets of these fascinating underground labyrinths." - Fatma, Historian and Tour Guide

In the end, Cappadocia is a place of endless adventure and discovery, just waiting to be explored. Whether you're soaring above the clouds in a hot air balloon, scaling the cliffs of Ihlara Valley, or riding horseback through Love Valley, the experiences and insights shared by locals offer a glimpse into the heart and soul of this magical land. So why not step off the beaten path and embark on your own Cappadocian adventure today?

Cappadocian Cuisine and Dining Experiences

TRADITIONAL TURKISH CUISINE

In the heart of Turkey lies Cappadocia, a region not only rich in history and natural wonders but also bursting with flavors that reflect its diverse cultural heritage. Traditional Turkish cuisine in Cappadocia is a culinary journey that tantalizes the taste buds and nourishes the soul, offering a delightful array of dishes that have been passed down through generations. From savory kebabs and hearty stews to delicate pastries and sweet treats, here are some highlights of Cappadocia's traditional Turkish cuisine:

1. Gözleme:

A staple of Turkish cuisine, gözleme is a savory pastry made from thin layers of dough that are rolled out and filled with a variety of ingredients such as cheese, spinach, potatoes, or minced meat. The filled dough is then folded over and cooked on a griddle until golden brown and crispy, resulting in a delicious and satisfying snack or meal.

2. Testi Kebabı:

Testi kebabı, or "pottery kebab," is a traditional Turkish dish that originated in Cappadocia. It consists of tender chunks of meat (usually lamb or beef) that are marinated in a rich blend of spices, then cooked slowly in a clay pot called a testi. The pot is sealed with dough to trap the flavors and juices inside, creating a succulent and aromatic dish that is typically served with rice or bread.

3. Mantı:

Mantı is a classic Turkish dumpling dish that is similar to ravioli or tortellini. The dumplings are filled with a savory mixture of spiced meat (usually lamb or beef) and onions, then boiled until tender. They are typically served with a garlic-yogurt sauce and drizzled with melted butter and a sprinkle of red pepper flakes, creating a rich and indulgent dish that is both comforting and delicious.

4. Meze:

Meze refers to a variety of small dishes that are served as appetizers or starters in Turkish cuisine. These can include a wide range of dishes such as hummus, tabbouleh, stuffed grape leaves, grilled vegetables, and more. Meze are typically served family-style, allowing diners to sample a variety of flavors and textures in one meal.

5. Baklava:

No discussion of Turkish cuisine would be complete without mentioning baklava, a decadent dessert made from layers of thin pastry dough, filled with chopped nuts (usually pistachios, walnuts, or almonds), and sweetened with syrup or honey. The layers are baked until golden and crispy, then drenched in a sweet syrup flavored with rose water or orange blossom water. The result is a rich and indulgent treat that is both crunchy and syrupy sweet, making it the perfect way to end a meal in Cappadocia.

In Cappadocia, traditional Turkish cuisine is more than just food—it's a celebration of culture, heritage, and hospitality. Whether you're sampling savory gözleme from a street vendor, savoring the rich flavors of testi kebabı at a local restaurant, or indulging in sweet baklava at a family-run bakery, every bite tells a story of tradition and craftsmanship that has been passed down through generations. So come hungry, bring an adventurous palate, and get ready to embark on a culinary journey through the flavors of Cappadocia.

LOCAL SPECIALTIES AND DISHES TO TRY

Cappadocia, with its rich cultural heritage and diverse culinary traditions, offers visitors a tantalizing array of local specialties and dishes that reflect the region's unique flavors and influences. From savory kebabs and hearty stews to delicate pastries and sweet treats, here are some must-try dishes and specialties that will take your taste buds on a delicious journey through Cappadocia:

1. Pottery Kebab (Testi Kebabı):

Originating from Cappadocia, pottery kebab is a signature dish that combines tender chunks of meat (typically lamb or beef) with an aromatic blend of spices. The meat is marinated, then slow-cooked in a clay pot called a "testi" until it becomes meltingly tender. The pot is sealed with dough before cooking, creating a succulent and flavorful dish that is as visually impressive as it is delicious.

2. Gözleme:

A beloved Turkish street food, gözleme is a savory flatbread made from thinly rolled dough that is filled with various ingredients such as cheese, spinach, potatoes, or minced meat. The filled dough is then folded over and cooked on a griddle until golden brown and crispy. Served hot off the grill, gözleme makes for a satisfying and portable snack or meal that's perfect for on-the-go dining.

3. Mantı:

Mantı is a traditional Turkish dumpling dish that features small pockets of dough filled with a savory mixture of spiced meat (usually lamb or beef) and onions. The dumplings are boiled until tender, then served topped with a garlic-yogurt sauce and drizzled with melted butter and a sprinkle of red pepper flakes. Mantı is a comfort food favorite in Cappadocia, known for its rich flavors and satisfying texture.

4. Şiş Kebab:

Şiş kebab, or skewered kebab, is a classic Turkish dish that features marinated chunks of meat (often lamb, beef, or chicken) grilled to perfection on skewers. The meat is typically seasoned with a blend of spices and served alongside grilled vegetables, rice, and a side of tangy yogurt sauce. Şiş kebab is a popular choice for both locals and visitors alike, offering a hearty and flavorful dining experience.

5. Sweets and Desserts:

No visit to Cappadocia would be complete without indulging in some of the region's delicious sweets and desserts. Baklava, a flaky pastry filled with nuts and sweetened with syrup or honey, is a perennial favorite, while künefe, a dessert made from shredded pastry soaked in syrup and layered with cheese, is another must-try treat. Other popular sweets include lokma (deep-fried dough balls soaked in syrup) and güllaç (a milk pudding dessert made with layers of pastry sheets and rose water).

6. Turkish Breakfast (Kahvaltı):

Start your day like a local with a traditional Turkish breakfast, or kahvaltı, which typically includes a variety of cheeses, olives, tomatoes, cucumbers, jams, honey, and freshly baked bread. Don't miss out on trying menemen, a flavorful egg dish cooked with tomatoes, peppers, and spices, or sucuk, a spicy Turkish sausage that packs a punch of flavor.

In Cappadocia, every meal is an opportunity to discover the region's rich culinary heritage and savor the unique flavors that have been perfected over centuries. So be sure to indulge in these local specialties and dishes during your visit—you won't be disappointed!

BEST RESTAURANTS AND CAFES IN CAPPADOCIA'

Cappadocia's vibrant culinary scene is a testament to the region's rich history and cultural diversity, offering visitors a delightful array of dining options that showcase traditional Turkish flavors as well as innovative twists on classic dishes. Whether you're craving authentic local cuisine, international fare, or a cozy cafe to unwind, here are some of the best restaurants and cafes in Cappadocia to satisfy your culinary cravings:

1. Topdeck Cave Restaurant (Göreme):

Perched atop a historic cave dwelling in Göreme, Topdeck Cave Restaurant offers diners panoramic views of the surrounding valleys and fairy chimneys while indulging in delicious Turkish cuisine. Known for its warm hospitality and charming ambiance, this restaurant serves up a variety of traditional dishes such as pottery kebab, gözleme, and meze platters, all made with fresh, locally sourced ingredients.

2. Ziggy's Shoppe & Cafe (Ürgüp):

Located in the heart of Ürgüp, Ziggy's Shoppe & Cafe is a cozy spot known for its relaxed atmosphere and delicious homemade fare. Serving up a mix of Turkish and international dishes, as well as freshly brewed coffee and homemade desserts, this cafe is the perfect place to refuel after a day of exploring Cappadocia's sights and attractions.

3. Old Greek House Restaurant (Mustafapaşa):

Housed in a beautifully restored Greek mansion in the charming village of Mustafapaşa, Old Greek House Restaurant offers diners an elegant setting to enjoy traditional Turkish cuisine with a modern twist. From flavorful kebabs and hearty stews to fresh salads and meze platters, every dish is prepared with care and attention to detail, ensuring a memorable dining experience.

4. Dibek Restaurant (Avanos):

Situated in the historic town of Avanos, Dibek Restaurant is a hidden gem known for its delicious Turkish home cooking and warm hospitality. The restaurant takes its name from the traditional "dibek" pots used to cook slow-cooked dishes, such as testi kebab and çömlek kebab, resulting in tender and flavorful meals that are sure to satisfy any appetite.

5. Kale Terasse Restaurant (Uçhisar):

Perched on the edge of Uçhisar Castle, Kale Terasse Restaurant offers diners stunning views of the surrounding valleys and mountains while enjoying a delicious meal. Specializing in traditional Turkish cuisine with a modern twist, this restaurant prides itself on using fresh, locally sourced ingredients to create dishes that are as visually stunning as they are flavorful.

6. Fırın Café & Bakery (Göreme):

For a taste of Cappadocia's sweet side, head to Fırın Café & Bakery in Göreme, where you'll find a tempting array of freshly baked pastries, cakes, and desserts. From flaky baklava and creamy künefe to indulgent chocolate cakes and fruity tarts, there's something to satisfy every sweet tooth at this charming cafe.

Whether you're craving classic Turkish flavors, international cuisine, or a sweet treat to indulge in, Cappadocia's restaurants and cafes offer a culinary experience that is sure to delight and inspire. So be sure to explore these culinary hotspots during your visit to Cappadocia—you won't be disappointed!

LOCAL INSIGHTS: FOOD STORIES AND FAVORITE DINING SPOTS SHARED BY LOCALS

In Cappadocia, food isn't just sustenance—it's a way of life. From hearty stews simmered for hours to delicate pastries passed down through generations, every dish tells a story of tradition, heritage, and the love that goes into preparing it. Here are some food stories and favorite dining spots shared by Cappadocian locals, offering a glimpse into the rich culinary tapestry of this enchanting region:

1. Mehmet's Pottery Kebab at Home:

"For me, there's nothing quite like the taste of my mother's pottery kebab, slow-cooked in a clay pot until the meat is fall-apart tender and infused with aromatic spices. It's a dish that brings our family together, reminding us of our shared heritage and the flavors of home. Whenever I'm craving a taste of comfort and nostalgia, I head to my mother's kitchen, where she still cooks up her signature pottery kebab with love and care."

2. Ayşe's Hidden Gem in Ürgüp:

"Growing up in Ürgüp, I've had the pleasure of discovering some of the best-kept secrets in Cappadocia's culinary scene. One of my favorite spots to dine is a small family-owned restaurant tucked away in the back streets of the town. Here, the chef serves up traditional Turkish dishes with a modern twist, using locally sourced ingredients and seasonal produce to create innovative and flavorful meals that never fail to impress. It's a hidden gem that I love to share with friends and visitors alike."

3. Mustafa's Morning Ritual at the Local Cafe:

"Every morning, I start my day with a strong cup of Turkish coffee and a freshly baked simit at my favorite local cafe. It's a ritual that I've been following for as long as I can remember—a moment of quiet reflection and connection with my community before the hustle and bustle of the day begins. The aroma of freshly brewed coffee and the warm, chewy texture of the simit never fail to put a smile on my face and set the tone for a great day ahead."

4. Fatma's Culinary Tour of Avanos:

"As a tour guide, I have the privilege of introducing visitors to the culinary delights of Cappadocia, and one of my favorite stops is the historic town of Avanos. Here, we explore the bustling bazaars and hidden backstreets, sampling local specialties such as testi kebab, çömlek kebab, and pottery-cooked dishes that are unique to the region. It's a culinary journey that celebrates the flavors, traditions, and stories of Cappadocia's rich cultural heritage."

5. Deniz's Sweet Tooth in Göreme:

"After a long day of exploring the sights and sounds of Göreme, there's nothing I love more than indulging in a sweet treat at my favorite bakery. Here, the aroma of freshly baked pastries fills the air, tempting passersby with the promise of flaky baklava, creamy künefe, and decadent chocolate cakes. It's a slice of heaven that satisfies my sweet tooth and brings a touch of joy to my day."

In Cappadocia, food is more than just nourishment—it's a celebration of life, family, and community. From cherished family recipes passed down through generations to hidden dining spots beloved by locals, every meal tells a story of tradition, culture, and the shared love of good food. So why not join us at the table and experience the flavors of Cappadocia for yourself?

Shopping in Cappadocia

SOUVENIRS AND HANDICRAFTS

Cappadocia isn't just a place to explore; it's a treasure trove of artisanal crafts and unique souvenirs waiting to be discovered. From intricately woven carpets and hand-painted ceramics to delicate textiles and exquisite jewelry, the region's rich cultural heritage is reflected in its diverse array of handicrafts. Whether you're searching for the perfect memento of your trip or looking to support local artisans, here are some of the most popular souvenirs and handicrafts to bring home from Cappadocia:

1. Turkish Carpets and Kilims:

No visit to Cappadocia would be complete without admiring the stunning Turkish carpets and kilims that adorn the region's bazaars and shops. Hand-woven by skilled artisans using traditional techniques passed down through generations, these carpets are prized for their intricate designs, vibrant colors, and luxurious textures. Whether you're drawn to the geometric patterns of Anatolian kilims or the rich hues of Turkish carpets, purchasing a carpet or kilim is a timeless souvenir that will add a touch of elegance and warmth to any home.

2. Cappadocian Pottery and Ceramics:

Cappadocia is renowned for its exquisite pottery and ceramics, which are characterized by their unique shapes, intricate designs, and vibrant colors. From traditional hand-painted plates and bowls to decorative vases and figurines, the region's pottery reflects the rich cultural heritage and artistic traditions of Cappadocia. Many shops and studios in towns like Avanos offer visitors the opportunity to watch skilled potters at work and even try their hand at creating their own pottery masterpiece.

3. Turkish Delight and Lokum:

Sweeten your memories of Cappadocia with a box of Turkish delight, or "lokum," a beloved confection made from sugar, starch, and flavorings such as rosewater, pistachio, or lemon. Available in a variety of shapes, colors, and flavors, Turkish delight is a popular souvenir that's perfect for sharing with friends and family back home. Look for shops and stalls selling freshly made lokum in flavors unique to Cappadocia, such as pomegranate, apricot, and walnut.

4. Handcrafted Textiles and Fabrics:

Immerse yourself in Cappadocia's rich textile tradition with a selection of handcrafted textiles and fabrics, including intricately woven rugs, embroidered pillow covers, and colorful scarves and shawls. Made from locally sourced materials such as wool, silk, and cotton, these textiles showcase the region's skilled craftsmanship and artistic flair. Whether you're searching for a statement piece for your wardrobe or a decorative accent for your home, Cappadocia's textiles offer a vibrant and stylish reminder of your travels.

5. Handmade Jewelry and Silverwork:

Elevate your style with a piece of handmade jewelry or silverwork inspired by the beauty of Cappadocia. From intricately designed earrings and necklaces to statement rings and bracelets, the region's jewelry reflects a blend of traditional motifs and contemporary styles. Look for shops and boutiques offering locally made jewelry crafted by skilled artisans using techniques passed down through generations, ensuring each piece is a unique and timeless treasure.

6. Local Art and Paintings:

Capture the essence of Cappadocia's stunning landscapes and vibrant culture with a piece of local art or painting. Many artists in the region draw inspiration from the region's surreal rock formations, ancient cave dwellings, and colorful hot air balloons, creating breathtaking works of art that capture the beauty and spirit of Cappadocia. Whether you prefer a traditional oil painting, a modern abstract piece, or a whimsical watercolor, purchasing a piece of local art is a wonderful way to bring a piece of Cappadocia's magic home with you.

In Cappadocia, every souvenir tells a story—a story of tradition, craftsmanship, and the enduring beauty of this enchanting region. So why not take home a piece of Cappadocia's rich cultural heritage and create lasting memories of your unforgettable journey?

POTTERY AND CERAMICS

Cappadocia's pottery and ceramics are not just objects; they are expressions of a rich cultural heritage that spans millennia. Rooted in the region's natural resources and artistic traditions, Cappadocian pottery and ceramics are renowned for their exquisite craftsmanship, intricate designs, and vibrant colors. From traditional earthenware vessels to decorative tiles and figurines, here's a glimpse into the captivating world of pottery and ceramics in Cappadocia:

1. Avanos: The Heart of Pottery Making

At the heart of Cappadocia's pottery scene lies the historic town of Avanos, where the tradition of pottery making has thrived for centuries. Situated on the banks of the Kızılırmak River, Avanos is known for its rich clay deposits, which have provided artisans with the raw materials needed to create their masterpieces. Visitors to

Avanos can explore the town's numerous pottery workshops and studios, where skilled artisans demonstrate age-old techniques such as throwing on a potter's wheel, hand-painting intricate designs, and firing pottery in traditional kilns.

2. Unique Designs and Techniques

Cappadocian pottery and ceramics are celebrated for their unique designs and techniques, which reflect the region's cultural diversity and artistic influences. From the whimsical motifs of Anatolian folklore to the geometric patterns of Islamic art, Cappadocia's pottery and ceramics showcase a rich tapestry of styles and aesthetics. Artisans often incorporate local motifs such as grapevines, pomegranates, and stylized animals into their designs, paying homage to the region's agricultural heritage and natural beauty.

3. Pottery Classes and Workshops

For those eager to try their hand at pottery making, Cappadocia offers a range of hands-on experiences and workshops where visitors can learn the art of pottery from skilled artisans. Whether you're a beginner or an experienced potter, these classes provide a unique opportunity to immerse yourself in Cappadocia's rich artistic heritage and create your own masterpiece to take home as a souvenir.

4. Decorative Tiles and Mosaics

In addition to functional pottery vessels, Cappadocian artisans are renowned for their decorative tiles and mosaics, which adorn the walls of historic buildings, mosques, and public spaces throughout the region. These intricately crafted tiles feature a kaleidoscope of colors and patterns, from floral motifs and arabesques to calligraphic inscriptions and geometric designs. Whether used as architectural elements or decorative accents, Cappadocia's tiles and mosaics add a touch of elegance and beauty to any environment.

5. Souvenirs and Keepsakes

From intricately painted plates and bowls to charming figurines and ornaments, Cappadocian pottery and ceramics make for unique and memorable souvenirs. Visitors to the region can browse the numerous shops and boutiques in towns like Avanos, Göreme, and Ürgüp, where they'll find a wide selection of pottery and ceramics ranging from traditional to contemporary styles. Whether you're searching for a practical piece of tableware or a decorative accent for your home, Cappadocia's pottery and ceramics offer something for every taste and budget.

In Cappadocia, pottery and ceramics are more than just objects; they are living expressions of a rich cultural heritage and artistic tradition that continues to thrive to this day. So why not explore the world of

Cappadocian pottery and ceramics during your visit to this enchanting region? Whether you're admiring the craftsmanship of local artisans, learning the art of pottery making yourself, or bringing home a piece of Cappadocia's beauty as a souvenir, you're sure to be captivated by the timeless allure of pottery and ceramics in Cappadocia.

CARPETS AND TEXTILES

Cappadocia, a land of enchanting landscapes and ancient traditions, is also renowned for its exquisite carpets and textiles. Woven with skill and passion by local artisans, these carpets and textiles reflect the region's rich cultural heritage and timeless beauty. From intricately patterned rugs to vibrant textiles, here's a glimpse into the captivating world of carpets and textiles in Cappadocia:

1. Anatolian Rugs:

Anatolian rugs are perhaps the most iconic symbol of Turkish craftsmanship, and Cappadocia is no exception. Handwoven by skilled artisans using traditional techniques passed down through generations, these rugs are prized for their intricate designs, rich colors, and luxurious textures. Whether adorned with geometric patterns, floral motifs, or symbolic motifs, Anatolian rugs are a testament to the region's artistic heritage and cultural diversity.

2. Kilims:

Kilims are another traditional form of woven textile that holds a special place in Cappadocia's cultural landscape. Made from wool or cotton, kilims are characterized by their flat-woven construction and bold geometric patterns. Used as floor coverings, wall hangings, or even bags and cushions, kilims are versatile and practical, yet also imbued with a sense of artistry and craftsmanship that speaks to the skill of the weaver.

3. Natural Dyes and Materials:

Many of the carpets and textiles produced in Cappadocia are made using natural dyes and materials sourced from the region's rich natural environment. Wool from local sheep is spun and dyed using plants, minerals, and insects found in the surrounding countryside, resulting in a vibrant palette of colors that range from earthy browns and greens to vivid reds, blues, and yellows. These natural dyes not only create beautiful hues but also ensure that each carpet and textile is unique and environmentally friendly.

4. Weaving Workshops and Demonstrations:

Visitors to Cappadocia can immerse themselves in the art of carpet weaving by visiting one of the many weaving workshops and studios scattered throughout the region. Here, skilled artisans demonstrate traditional weaving techniques, from spinning and dyeing the wool to setting up the loom and creating intricate patterns. Visitors can also try their hand at weaving under the guidance of experienced weavers, gaining a deeper appreciation for the skill and artistry involved in creating these timeless treasures.

5. Souvenirs and Keepsakes:

Whether you're searching for a practical floor covering, a decorative wall hanging, or a unique souvenir to bring home from your travels, Cappadocia's carpets and textiles offer something for every taste and budget. Visitors can browse the numerous shops and boutiques in towns like Göreme, Ürgüp, and Avanos, where they'll find a wide selection of rugs, kilims, cushions, and other textile products, each one a testament to the region's rich cultural heritage and artistic tradition.

In Cappadocia, carpets and textiles are more than just functional objects; they are works of art that tell a story of craftsmanship, tradition, and cultural identity. Whether you're admiring the intricate patterns of an Anatolian rug, learning the art of weaving from a skilled artisan, or bringing home a piece of Cappadocia's beauty as a souvenir, you're sure to be captivated by the timeless allure of carpets and textiles in this enchanting region.

LOCAL INSIGHTS: ARTISANS' STORIES AND INSIDER TIPS ON WHERE TO FIND AUTHENTIC LOCAL CRAFTS

In the heart of Cappadocia's charming towns and villages, a rich tradition of craftsmanship has been passed down through generations. From skilled rug weavers to talented pottery makers, local artisans play a vital role in preserving the region's cultural heritage and creating unique works of art that reflect Cappadocia's timeless beauty. Here are some insights and insider tips from these artisans themselves, along with recommendations on where to find authentic local crafts:

1. Ahmet, Master Rug Weaver:

"For me, rug weaving is not just a craft—it's a way of life that connects me to my ancestors and the rich cultural heritage of Cappadocia. Each rug tells a story, from the natural dyes and materials used to the intricate patterns and motifs woven into its design. Visitors to Cappadocia can experience the art of rug weaving firsthand by visiting our workshop in Avanos, where they can watch us at work and learn about the time-honored techniques we use to create these timeless treasures."

Insider Tip: "For the best selection of authentic rugs and textiles, I recommend visiting the local bazaars and artisan markets in towns like Avanos and Göreme. Here, you'll find a wide variety of rugs, kilims, and other textile products handcrafted by local artisans, each one a unique reflection of Cappadocia's artistic heritage."

2. Fatma, Ceramic Artist:

"As a ceramic artist, I draw inspiration from the natural beauty and rich history of Cappadocia, incorporating traditional motifs and techniques into my work to create contemporary pieces that resonate with locals and visitors alike. Whether I'm hand-painting intricate designs on pottery or sculpting whimsical figurines from clay, each piece is infused with a sense of craftsmanship and creativity that is uniquely Cappadocian."

Insider Tip: "For those interested in exploring Cappadocia's pottery scene, I recommend visiting the pottery workshops and studios in Avanos, where you can watch skilled artisans at work and even try your hand at creating your own pottery masterpiece. Many workshops also offer guided tours and demonstrations, providing valuable insights into the art of pottery making in Cappadocia."

3. Mehmet, Master Carpet Weaver:

"Carpet weaving has been a part of my family's heritage for generations, and I take great pride in continuing this tradition in my workshop in Ürgüp. Using locally sourced wool and natural dyes, we create carpets and kilims that showcase the rich colors and intricate designs of Cappadocia's landscape and culture. Visitors to our workshop can witness the weaving process firsthand and learn about the history and significance of carpet weaving in Cappadocia."

Insider Tip: "To find authentic carpets and textiles in Cappadocia, I recommend seeking out the smaller, family-run shops and boutiques in towns like Ürgüp and Avanos. Here, you'll often find a more diverse selection of handmade rugs, kilims, and other textile products, along with the opportunity to interact directly with the artisans who create them."

4. Ayşe, Textile Designer:

"As a textile designer, I draw inspiration from the vibrant colors and patterns of Cappadocia's landscape, incorporating traditional weaving techniques and contemporary designs into my creations. Whether I'm hand-dyeing yarns, experimenting with different weaving styles, or designing new patterns, each piece is a labor of love that reflects my passion for Cappadocia's rich artistic heritage."

Insider Tip: "For a truly immersive experience, I recommend visiting one of the many textile workshops and studios in Cappadocia, where you can learn about the art of weaving from skilled artisans and even participate in hands-on workshops. Many workshops also offer guided tours and demonstrations, providing valuable insights into the techniques and traditions of textile making in Cappadocia."

In Cappadocia, the art of craftsmanship is alive and thriving, thanks to the dedication and talent of local artisans. Whether you're admiring the intricate patterns of a handmade rug, watching a potter at work in their studio, or exploring the vibrant textile scene in one of Cappadocia's workshops, you'll discover a world of creativity and tradition that is uniquely Cappadocian.

Cultural Experiences and Festivals

FOLK MUSIC AND DANCE PERFORMANCES

Cappadocia's cultural tapestry is woven with the vibrant threads of folk music and dance, a tradition that celebrates the region's rich history, folklore, and community spirit. From lively performances at local festivals to intimate gatherings in village squares, folk music and dance play an integral role in the social fabric of Cappadocia, bringing people together to share stories, laughter, and the joy of music. Here's a closer look at the captivating world of folk music and dance performances in Cappadocia:

1. Traditional Instruments:

The sound of folk music in Cappadocia is characterized by the melodies of traditional instruments such as the bağlama (a long-necked lute), the zurna (a double-reed wind instrument), and the davul (a large drum). These instruments, often handcrafted by local artisans, produce a rich and vibrant sound that forms the backbone of Cappadocia's musical traditions.

2. Melodic Tunes and Lively Rhythms:

Folk music in Cappadocia encompasses a wide range of styles and genres, from lively dance tunes to soulful ballads. Many of these songs are passed down through generations, telling stories of love, loss, and the beauty of life in Cappadocia. Whether performed by professional musicians on stage or shared spontaneously among friends and neighbors, folk music in Cappadocia is a celebration of the human experience in all its diversity.

3. Traditional Dances:

Accompanying the music are traditional dances that reflect the rhythm and spirit of Cappadocia's cultural heritage. One such dance is the "horon," a lively circle dance performed by both men and women, characterized by fast footwork and energetic movements. Another popular dance is the "halay," a line dance often performed at weddings and other celebrations, where dancers hold hands and move in unison to the beat of the music.

4. Festivals and Celebrations:

Throughout the year, Cappadocia comes alive with a variety of festivals and celebrations that showcase the region's folk music and dance traditions. From the annual grape harvest festival in Ürgüp to the traditional wedding ceremonies in villages like Göreme and Avanos, these events provide opportunities for locals and visitors alike to experience the joy and camaraderie of Cappadocia's cultural heritage.

5. Cultural Centers and Performances:

For those interested in experiencing folk music and dance performances in a more structured setting, Cappadocia's cultural centers and performance venues offer regular concerts and shows featuring local musicians and dancers. These performances often include demonstrations of traditional instruments, interactive workshops, and opportunities for audience participation, providing a deeper insight into the rhythms and melodies of Cappadocia's folk music traditions.

6. Authentic Experiences:

For a truly immersive experience, visitors to Cappadocia can seek out authentic folk music and dance performances in local villages and towns. Whether stumbled upon during a stroll through the streets or sought out intentionally at a traditional teahouse or restaurant, these impromptu performances offer glimpses into the heart and soul of Cappadocia's cultural identity, where music and dance are woven into the fabric of everyday life.

In Cappadocia, folk music and dance are more than just performances; they are expressions of a shared heritage and a celebration of community. Whether experienced at a lively festival, an intimate gathering, or a spontaneous street performance, the melodies and rhythms of Cappadocia's folk music and dance traditions have the power to inspire, uplift, and connect people across cultures and generations.

POTTERY WORKSHOPS

In the heart of Cappadocia's historic towns and villages, pottery workshops stand as living testaments to the region's rich tradition of craftsmanship and artistic expression. From the ancient techniques of clay shaping to the vibrant hues of hand-applied glazes, these workshops offer visitors a unique opportunity to immerse themselves in the art of pottery making and create their own ceramic masterpieces. Here's a closer look at the enchanting world of pottery workshops in Cappadocia:

1. Heritage of Avanos:

Avanos, a picturesque town nestled along the banks of the Kızılırmak River, is renowned as the pottery capital of Cappadocia. For centuries, artisans in Avanos have been shaping clay into beautiful vessels using techniques passed down through generations. Visitors to

Avanos can explore the town's numerous pottery workshops and studios, where skilled artisans welcome guests into their creative spaces and share the secrets of their craft.

2. Hands-on Experience:

One of the highlights of visiting a pottery workshop in Cappadocia is the opportunity to try your hand at pottery making yourself. Under the guidance of experienced potters, visitors can learn the basics of clay shaping, wheel throwing, and glazing, creating their own unique pieces to take home as souvenirs. Whether it's shaping a simple bowl or sculpting a decorative figurine, the hands-on experience of pottery making is both educational and deeply satisfying.

3. Traditional Techniques:

At the heart of pottery making in Cappadocia are the time-honored techniques that have been passed down through generations. Visitors to pottery workshops can watch skilled artisans demonstrate these techniques firsthand, from throwing clay on a potter's wheel to hand-painting intricate designs onto finished pieces. Many workshops also offer guided tours and demonstrations, providing valuable insights into the history and significance of pottery making in Cappadocia.

4. Creative Expression:

Pottery workshops in Cappadocia are not just about learning a craft; they're also about unleashing creativity and self-expression. Whether you're a novice or an experienced potter, the workshops provide a supportive environment where guests can explore their artistic instincts and create pottery pieces that reflect their own unique style and personality. From traditional designs to contemporary motifs, the possibilities are endless when it comes to pottery making in Cappadocia.

5. Souvenirs and Keepsakes:

After creating their own pottery pieces, visitors to pottery workshops in Cappadocia can take home their creations as cherished souvenirs of their time in the region. Whether it's a beautifully glazed bowl, a hand-painted plate, or a whimsical figurine, these handmade pottery pieces serve as tangible reminders of the memories and experiences shared during their visit to Cappadocia.

6. Cultural Immersion:

More than just a tourist activity, pottery workshops in Cappadocia offer visitors a deeper connection to the region's cultural heritage and artistic traditions. By learning about the history, techniques, and symbolism behind pottery making in Cappadocia, guests gain a greater appreciation for the craftsmanship and creativity that have shaped this ancient art form for centuries.

In Cappadocia, pottery workshops are not just places to learn a craft; they're gateways to a world of creativity, tradition, and cultural immersion. Whether you're shaping clay alongside skilled artisans, learning about the history and techniques of pottery making, or simply admiring the beauty of handmade ceramics, a visit to a pottery workshop in Cappadocia is sure to be a memorable and enriching experience.

CAPPADOCIA FESTIVALS AND EVENTS

Cappadocia, with its rich cultural heritage and stunning natural beauty, provides the perfect backdrop for a vibrant array of festivals and events throughout the year. From traditional celebrations steeped in folklore to contemporary cultural gatherings, these festivals offer visitors a unique opportunity to immerse themselves in the sights, sounds, and flavors of this enchanting region. Here's a glimpse into some of the most notable festivals and events in Cappadocia:

1. International Hot Air Balloon Festival:

Each year, thousands of visitors flock to Cappadocia for the International Hot Air Balloon Festival, one of the largest of its kind in the world. Against the backdrop of Cappadocia's surreal landscape, colorful balloons take to the sky in a breathtaking display of beauty and skill. Visitors can join in the festivities by taking a sunrise balloon ride or watching the spectacular mass ascents from the ground.

2. Grape Harvest Festival:

Held in the fall when the vineyards are heavy with ripe grapes, the Grape Harvest Festival is a celebration of Cappadocia's rich agricultural heritage. Visitors can participate in traditional grape-picking activities, sample locally produced wines and grape-based delicacies, and enjoy live music, dance performances, and cultural exhibitions showcasing the region's viticultural traditions.

3. Cappadox:

Cappadox is a unique cultural festival that celebrates the intersection of music, art, and nature in Cappadocia. Held annually in various locations across the region, Cappadox features an eclectic lineup of musical performances, art installations, workshops, and outdoor adventures such as hiking, biking, and yoga. Visitors can immerse themselves in the creative energy of Cappadox while exploring the stunning landscapes and cultural heritage of the region.

4. Camel Wrestling Festival:

A centuries-old tradition in Turkey, camel wrestling is a spectacle unlike any other, and the Camel Wrestling Festival in Cappadocia is one of the most popular events of its kind. Held during the winter months, the festival attracts crowds of spectators who gather to watch as adorned camels compete in wrestling matches to determine the strongest and most dominant champion.

5. Nevşehir International Music and Folk Dance Festival:

Organized by the Nevşehir Municipality, the International Music and Folk Dance Festival brings together performers from around the world to showcase their traditional music and dance. Visitors can enjoy colorful performances by dance troupes, musical ensembles, and cultural groups representing diverse cultures and traditions, creating a vibrant tapestry of global unity and artistic expression.

6. Traditional Turkish Night:

For those seeking an authentic taste of Turkish culture, a Traditional Turkish Night offers a feast for the senses. Hosted in venues throughout Cappadocia, these evenings feature live music, folk dances, and traditional Turkish cuisine, providing visitors with an immersive experience of Turkish hospitality and entertainment.

Whether you're soaring high above the landscape in a hot air balloon, stomping grapes at a harvest festival, or dancing the night away at a traditional Turkish celebration, festivals and events in Cappadocia offer a unique opportunity to connect with the region's rich cultural heritage and vibrant community spirit. So why not join in the festivities and create unforgettable memories in this captivating corner of Turkey?

LOCAL INSIGHTS: CULTURAL STORIES AND INTERVIEWS WITH ARTISTS AND PERFORMERS

In the heart of Cappadocia's enchanting towns and villages, a rich tapestry of culture and tradition unfolds, woven together by the talented artists and performers who call this region home. From skilled artisans crafting pottery to passionate musicians playing traditional melodies, these individuals are the guardians of Cappadocia's cultural heritage, keeping alive ancient traditions while infusing them with new life and creativity. Here are some captivating stories and insights from the artists and performers of Cappadocia:

1. Ayşe, Textile Designer:

"As a textile designer, I draw inspiration from the vibrant colors and patterns of Cappadocia's landscape, incorporating traditional weaving techniques and contemporary designs into my creations. Each piece I create tells a story—a story of the land, the people, and the cultural heritage that defines Cappadocia. Through my work, I hope to share the beauty and richness of this region with the world."

2. Mehmet, Master Carpet Weaver:

"For generations, my family has been weaving carpets in Cappadocia, passing down the art and tradition from one generation to the next. Each carpet we create is a labor of love, infused with the spirit of our ancestors and the rhythms of the land. Through our work, we strive to preserve the cultural heritage of Cappadocia and share it with others, so that future generations may continue to appreciate its beauty and significance."

3. Fatma, Ceramic Artist:

"For me, pottery is more than just a craft—it's a form of self-expression, a way of connecting with the earth and the elements. When I shape clay with my hands, I feel a deep connection to the land and the ancient traditions of Cappadocia. Through my pottery, I seek to capture the essence of this region—the colors, the textures, the stories that have shaped its identity for centuries."

4. Ahmet, Master Rug Weaver:

"Rug weaving is a part of my soul, a tradition that has been passed down through countless generations in Cappadocia. Each rug I weave is a tribute to the land and the people who have shaped my identity as an artist. Through my work, I hope to preserve the cultural heritage of Cappadocia and honor the craftsmanship of those who came before me."

5. Nazlı, Folk Musician:

"As a folk musician, I feel a deep connection to the melodies and rhythms of Cappadocia, passed down through generations in songs and stories. Through my music, I strive to keep alive the traditions of this region, sharing the joy and beauty of Cappadocian folk music with audiences near and far. For me, music is not just a performance—it's a celebration of culture, community, and connection."

6. Mustafa, Traditional Dancer:

"Growing up in Cappadocia, I was surrounded by the sights and sounds of traditional dance, from the lively horon to the graceful halay. For me, dance is a way of expressing my love for this region, of honoring the traditions and customs that have shaped my identity. Through my performances, I hope to share the joy and energy of Cappadocia's dance traditions with audiences around the world."

Through their artistry and passion, the artists and performers of Cappadocia breathe life into the region's cultural heritage, enriching the lives of locals and visitors alike. Their stories and insights offer a glimpse into the soul of Cappadocia, revealing the deep connections between art, tradition, and the land that inspires them.

Practical Tips for Traveling in Cappadocia

ESSENTIAL PACKING LIST

Packing for your adventure in Cappadocia? Here's your essential packing list to ensure you're prepared for all the experiences this captivating region has to offer:

1. Comfortable Footwear:

With its rugged terrain and multitude of trails to explore, comfortable footwear is a must. Pack sturdy hiking boots or walking shoes for exploring the valleys, hiking trails, and historical sites of Cappadocia.

2. Layered Clothing:

Cappadocia experiences varying temperatures throughout the day, so be sure to pack layered clothing to stay comfortable. Lightweight, breathable fabrics are ideal for daytime excursions, while warmer layers are essential for cooler evenings.

3. Sun Protection:

With its sunny climate, sun protection is essential in Cappadocia. Pack sunscreen with a high SPF, sunglasses to shield your eyes from the sun's glare, and a wide-brimmed hat to protect your face and neck.

4. Water Bottle:

Staying hydrated is key, especially when exploring the outdoors. Bring a refillable water bottle to stay refreshed throughout the day, and consider packing electrolyte tablets to replenish essential minerals lost through sweating.

5. Daypack:

A lightweight daypack is essential for carrying essentials such as water, snacks, sunscreen, and a camera while exploring Cappadocia's valleys and attractions. Look for a pack with padded straps and multiple compartments for added comfort and organization.

6. Camera or Smartphone:

Cappadocia's otherworldly landscapes and cultural attractions provide endless opportunities for photography. Don't forget to pack your camera or smartphone to capture memories of your adventures, from hot air balloon rides to historic sites and scenic vistas.

7. Power Adapter:

Ensure you can keep your devices charged by packing a universal power adapter suitable for Turkish electrical outlets. This will allow you to charge your electronics and stay connected throughout your stay in Cappadocia.

8. Travel Documents:

Don't forget to pack essential travel documents, including your passport, visa (if required), travel insurance details, and any reservations or tickets for activities and accommodations in Cappadocia.

9. Personal Toiletries:

Pack travel-sized toiletries, including shampoo, conditioner, body wash, toothpaste, and a toothbrush. Don't forget any medications or personal hygiene products you may need during your stay.

10. Cash and Credit Cards:

While many establishments in Cappadocia accept credit cards, it's a good idea to carry some cash for smaller purchases, tips, and transactions at local markets or street vendors.

11. Guidebook or Maps:

Bring along a guidebook or maps of Cappadocia to help you navigate the region's attractions, trails, and landmarks. This will also provide valuable information on local customs, culture, and points of interest.

12. Sense of Adventure:

Most importantly, pack a sense of adventure and openness to new experiences. Cappadocia is a land of wonders waiting to be discovered, and with the right mindset, you're sure to have an unforgettable journey.

With this essential packing list in hand, you're ready to embark on your adventure in Cappadocia and create memories that will last a lifetime. Safe travels!

Safety Tips

LOCAL ETIQUETTE AND CUSTOMS

Navigating local etiquette and customs is essential for a smooth and respectful experience while visiting Cappadocia. Here's a guide to help you understand and adhere to the cultural norms of the region:

1. Greetings and Politeness:

When meeting someone for the first time or entering a shop or restaurant, it's customary to greet with a handshake and a warm smile.

Use polite language and expressions, such as "Merhaba" (hello) and "Lütfen" (please), to show respect and courtesy.

2. Modest Dress:

While Turkey is generally a secular country, it's respectful to dress modestly, especially when visiting religious sites like mosques or monasteries. Avoid revealing clothing and cover your shoulders and knees.

Remove your shoes before entering mosques or homes as a sign of respect.

3. Dining Etiquette:

When dining in Cappadocia, it's common to share meals family-style. Wait for the host to invite you to begin eating before starting your meal.

Use your right hand for eating and greeting, as the left hand is considered unclean in Turkish culture.

If invited to someone's home for a meal, bring a small gift such as flowers or sweets as a token of appreciation.

4. Social Customs:

Turks are known for their hospitality and friendliness. Engage in conversations with locals, ask questions about their culture and traditions, and be open to making new connections.

Avoid discussing sensitive topics such as politics or religion, as these can be divisive subjects.

5. Respect for Elders:

In Turkish culture, respect for elders is highly valued. Use formal language and gestures when addressing older individuals, and defer to their opinions and preferences whenever possible.

6. Tipping:

Tipping is customary in Cappadocia, especially in restaurants, cafes, and hotels. A tip of around 10-15% of the total bill is appreciated for good service.

7. Public Behavior:

Public displays of affection are generally frowned upon in Turkish culture, so refrain from kissing or hugging in public.

Avoid raising your voice or engaging in confrontational behavior, as Turks value harmony and politeness in social interactions.

8. Photography Etiquette:

Always ask for permission before taking photos of individuals, especially in rural areas or religious sites.

Respect any signs or guidelines regarding photography at tourist attractions or cultural sites.

By adhering to these local etiquette and customs, you'll show respect for the culture and traditions of Cappadocia, fostering positive interactions and memorable experiences during your visit.

Local Phrases & Language Guide

Mastering a few key phrases in the local language can greatly enhance your experience while exploring Cappadocia. Here's a helpful language guide to get you started:

1. Basic Greetings:

Hello: Merhaba (MEHR-hah-bah)

Good morning: Günaydın (GOO-nahy-duhn)

Good afternoon/evening: İyi akşamlar (EE-yee AHK-shahm-lahr)

Goodbye: Hoşça kalın (HOSH-chah kah-LUHN)

Thank you: Teşekkür ederim (teh-SHEHK-kyoor eh-deh-REEM)

You're welcome: Rica ederim (REE-jah eh-deh-REEM)

2. Polite Expressions:

Please: Lütfen (LUTFEHN)

Excuse me: Affedersiniz (ahf-feh-dehr-SEE-NEEZ)

I'm sorry: Üzgünüm (OOZ-goon-oom)

3. Basic Questions:

Yes: Evet (EH-veht)

No: Hayır (HA-yuhr)

How are you?: Nasılsınız? (NAH-suhl-suh-NUHZ?)

What is your name?: Adınız nedir? (AH-duh-nuhz NEH-deer?)

Where is...?: ...nerede? (...neh-REH-deh?)

4. Directions and Transportation:

Where is the bus station?: Otobüs durağı nerede? (oh-toh-BUSS doo-RAH-uh neh-REH-deh?)

How much is this?: Bu ne kadar? (boo neh KAHD-ahr?)

Where is the restroom?: Tuvalet nerede? (too-vah-LEHT neh-REH-deh?)

I need a taxi: Taksiye ihtiyacım var (TAHK-see-yeh eeht-YAH-juhm vahr)

5. Food and Dining:

I would like...: ...istiyorum (...ees-tee-YOH-room)

Water: Su (soo)

Bread: Ekmek (ehk-MEHK)

Delicious: Lezzetli (LEH-zehht-lee)

Cheers!: Şerefe! (SHEH-reh-feh)

6. Emergencies:

Help!: Yardım edin! (YAR-duhm eh-DEEN)

I need a doctor: Doktora ihtiyacım var (DOHK-toh-rah eeht-YAH-juhm vahr)

Call the police: Polisi arayın (poh-LEE-see ah-rah-YUHN)

7. Numbers:

1: Bir (beer)

2: İki (ee-kee)

3: Üç (oosh)

4: Dört (dohrt)

5: Beş (besh)

10: On (ohn)

Practice these phrases before your trip, and don't hesitate to use them during your time in Cappadocia. Locals will appreciate your effort to communicate in their language, and it will likely lead to more enjoyable interactions and experiences.

Day Trips and Excursions from Cappadocia

IHLARA VALLEY

Nestled amidst the rugged landscape of Cappadocia lies the breathtaking Ihlara Valley, a hidden gem waiting to be discovered by adventurous travelers. Carved by the Melendiz River over millions of years, this lush canyon stretches for approximately 14 kilometers (8.7 miles) and offers visitors a unique blend of natural beauty, cultural heritage, and outdoor adventure. Here's what you need to know about exploring the enchanting Ihlara Valley:

1. Natural Wonders:

The Ihlara Valley is renowned for its stunning natural scenery, characterized by towering rock formations, verdant vegetation, and meandering streams. As you hike along the valley floor, you'll encounter towering cliffs, tranquil ponds, and hidden waterfalls, creating a picturesque landscape that is sure to leave you awe-struck.

2. Rich History:

In addition to its natural beauty, the Ihlara Valley is also home to numerous historical and cultural sites dating back thousands of years. Along the canyon walls, you'll find ancient rock-cut churches, chapels, and monasteries carved into the soft volcanic tuff, adorned with intricate frescoes depicting scenes from the life of Jesus Christ and biblical stories. These remarkable religious sites provide a fascinating glimpse into Cappadocia's rich Byzantine heritage.

3. Hiking and Exploration:

The Ihlara Valley offers excellent opportunities for hiking and exploration, with well-marked trails that wind their way along the canyon floor and through its rugged terrain. Whether you're a seasoned hiker or a casual nature enthusiast, there are trails of varying lengths and difficulty levels to suit every skill level. Along the way, you'll encounter breathtaking viewpoints, hidden caves, and archaeological ruins, making each step of the journey a memorable experience.

4. Cultural Encounters:

As you explore the Ihlara Valley, you'll have the opportunity to interact with local villagers and gain insight into their traditional way of life. Along the trail, you'll find charming villages where you can stop for a refreshing glass of çay (Turkish tea) or sample delicious local cuisine at a rustic taverna. Take the time to chat with the friendly locals and learn about their customs, traditions, and livelihoods—it's these authentic cultural encounters that make the journey truly memorable.

5. Practical Tips:

Wear sturdy hiking shoes and comfortable clothing suitable for outdoor exploration.

Bring plenty of water, sunscreen, and a hat to protect yourself from the sun.

Start your hike early in the day to avoid the midday heat and crowds.

Pack a camera to capture the stunning scenery and historic landmarks along the way.

Consider hiring a local guide to enhance your experience and learn more about the valley's history and natural features.

The Ihlara Valley offers a perfect blend of natural beauty, cultural heritage, and outdoor adventure, making it a must-visit destination for travelers to Cappadocia. Whether you're exploring ancient churches, hiking along scenic trails, or simply soaking in the serenity of the canyon, a visit to the Ihlara Valley is sure to be a highlight of your journey through this enchanting region.

Avanos Town

Nestled along the banks of the Kızılırmak River, Avanos exudes a timeless charm that captivates visitors with its rich history, vibrant culture, and stunning natural beauty. Known as the pottery capital of Cappadocia, this picturesque town offers a unique blend of artistic tradition, local craftsmanship, and warm hospitality. Here's what you need to know about exploring the enchanting town of Avanos:

1. Pottery Tradition:

Avanos has been synonymous with pottery making for centuries, thanks to its abundant clay deposits and skilled artisans who have perfected the craft over generations. Wander through the cobblestone streets of the town, and you'll encounter numerous pottery workshops and studios where you can watch master potters at work, shaping clay into exquisite vessels using traditional techniques passed down through the ages.

2. Hands-on Workshops:

One of the highlights of visiting Avanos is the opportunity to try your hand at pottery making yourself. Many workshops offer hands-on classes where visitors can learn the basics of clay shaping, wheel throwing, and glazing under the guidance of experienced artisans. It's a chance to unleash your creativity and create your own unique pottery masterpiece to take home as a souvenir of your time in Avanos.

3. Cultural Heritage:

Beyond its pottery tradition, Avanos is steeped in history and culture, with roots dating back to ancient times. Explore the town's historic landmarks, including the Avanos Castle, which offers panoramic views of the surrounding landscape, and the Seljuk-era caravanserai, where travelers once rested along the Silk Road. Don't miss the opportunity to visit the Avanos Hair Museum, where thousands of locks of hair from female visitors around the world are displayed as a quirky tribute to the town's cultural heritage.

4. Riverside Serenity:

The tranquil waters of the Kızılırmak River add to the charm of Avanos, providing a picturesque backdrop for leisurely strolls and outdoor activities. Take a relaxing boat ride along the river, or simply find a quiet spot along the riverbank to soak in the serenity and natural beauty of the surroundings.

5. Local Cuisine:

No visit to Avanos would be complete without sampling the local cuisine. Head to one of the town's charming tavernas or family-run restaurants to savor authentic Turkish dishes made with fresh, locally sourced ingredients. Be sure to try specialties such as mantı (Turkish dumplings), testi kebabı (clay pot kebab), and gözleme (savory Turkish pancakes) for a true taste of Cappadocian cuisine.

6. Artisanal Souvenirs:

In addition to pottery, Avanos is also known for its artisanal handicrafts, including handwoven carpets, textiles, and jewelry. Browse the town's bustling bazaars and boutique shops to find unique souvenirs and gifts to take home, each crafted with the same care and attention to detail that defines Avanos' artistic tradition.

From its storied pottery workshops to its historic landmarks and riverside charm,

Avanos invites visitors to immerse themselves in the rich tapestry of Cappadocian culture and craftsmanship. Whether you're shaping clay alongside master potters, exploring ancient landmarks, or simply savoring the flavors of local cuisine, a visit to Avanos is sure to leave a lasting impression and create memories to treasure for years to come.

SOGANLI VALLEY

Nestled amidst the rugged landscape of Cappadocia, Soganli Valley stands as a serene oasis of natural beauty and ancient history, beckoning travelers to explore its hidden wonders. Tucked away from the bustling tourist trails, this tranquil valley offers a peaceful retreat where visitors can immerse themselves in the breathtaking scenery, discover ancient rock-cut churches, and connect with the timeless rhythms of rural life. Here's what you need to know about exploring the enchanting Soganli Valley:

1. Spectacular Scenery:

Soganli Valley captivates visitors with its stunning natural beauty, characterized by towering rock formations, verdant vineyards, and fertile orchards. As you wander along the valley floor, you'll be surrounded by a kaleidoscope of colors, from the vibrant green of the vegetation to the warm hues of the rocky cliffs, creating a picturesque landscape that is sure to leave you spellbound.

2. Ancient Rock-Cut Churches:

One of the highlights of Soganli Valley is its impressive collection of rock-cut churches and monasteries, which date back to the Byzantine era. Carved into the soft volcanic tuff, these ancient sanctuaries are adorned with intricate frescoes depicting scenes from the life of Jesus Christ, biblical stories, and symbolic motifs. Explore the valley's network of hiking trails to discover hidden gems such as the Karabas Kilise (Black Church) and the Yilanli Kilise (Snake Church), each offering a glimpse into Cappadocia's rich religious heritage.

3. Rural Life and Local Culture:

Soganli Valley provides a rare opportunity to experience the traditional way of life in rural Cappadocia. Along the way, you'll encounter charming villages where time seems to stand still, with stone houses, ancient churches, and terraced fields dotting the landscape. Take the time to chat with local villagers, learn about their customs and traditions, and perhaps even sample homemade treats such as fresh fruit, olives, and traditional gözleme (Turkish pancakes).

4. Outdoor Adventures:

For outdoor enthusiasts, Soganli Valley offers excellent opportunities for hiking, photography, and birdwatching. Follow the well-marked hiking trails that crisscross the valley, leading you past ancient landmarks, scenic viewpoints, and hidden caves waiting to be explored. Keep an eye out for the diverse wildlife that calls the valley home, including birds of prey, wildflowers, and butterflies.

5. Practical Tips:

Wear sturdy hiking shoes and comfortable clothing suitable for outdoor exploration.

Bring plenty of water, sunscreen, and a hat to protect yourself from the sun.

Respect the cultural and religious significance of the rock-cut churches, and refrain from touching or damaging the frescoes.

Consider hiring a local guide to enhance your experience and learn more about the history and natural features of Soganli Valley.

Whether you're marveling at ancient frescoes, meandering through picturesque villages, or simply soaking in the tranquility of the countryside, a visit to Soganli Valley is sure to be a highlight of your journey through Cappadocia. So lace up your hiking boots, pack your camera, and prepare to be enchanted by the timeless beauty of this hidden gem in the heart of Turkey.

MOUNT ERCIYES SKI RESORT

Nestled majestically in the heart of Central Anatolia, Mount Erciyes stands as a towering sentinel, beckoning winter sports enthusiasts to its snowy slopes. Renowned as one of Turkey's premier ski destinations, Mount Erciyes Ski Resort offers an unforgettable alpine experience, boasting pristine powder, exhilarating runs, and breathtaking vistas. Here's what you need to know to make the most of your visit to this winter wonderland:

1. Skiing and Snowboarding:

With its vast expanse of skiable terrain and diverse range of slopes catering to all skill levels, Mount Erciyes Ski Resort offers endless opportunities for skiing and snowboarding enthusiasts. From gentle beginner slopes to challenging black diamond runs, there's something for everyone to enjoy. Rent top-quality equipment from the resort's rental shops or sign up for lessons with certified instructors to improve your skills and confidence on the snow.

2. Snow Conditions:

Situated at an altitude of over 3,900 meters (12,800 feet), Mount Erciyes enjoys abundant snowfall throughout the winter season, typically from December to April. The resort's high elevation ensures excellent snow conditions, with soft powder and well-groomed trails ideal for carving turns and cruising down the mountain. Check the resort's website or inquire locally for up-to-date information on snow conditions and weather forecasts before your visit.

3. Scenic Chairlift Rides:

For those who prefer to take in the stunning scenery without hitting the slopes, Mount Erciyes Ski Resort offers scenic chairlift rides that provide panoramic views of the surrounding mountains and valleys. Sit back, relax, and soak in the breathtaking vistas as you glide effortlessly above the snow-covered landscape, capturing memorable photos of your mountain adventure.

4. Après-Ski Activities:

After a day on the slopes, unwind and indulge in the resort's après-ski offerings, which include cozy mountain lodges, inviting cafés, and lively bars where you can warm up by the fire, sip on hot beverages, and mingle with fellow skiers and snowboarders. Treat yourself to hearty Turkish cuisine and regional specialties, such as köfte (grilled meatballs), kebabs, and pide (Turkish pizza), for a satisfying end to your day on the mountain.

5. Accommodation Options:

Mount Erciyes Ski Resort offers a range of accommodation options to suit every budget and preference, from luxury hotels and cozy chalets to budget-friendly guesthouses and hostels. Stay slopeside for convenient access to the lifts and amenities, or opt for accommodation in nearby towns such as Kayseri or Develi for a quieter retreat away from the crowds.

6. Safety Tips:

Always ski or snowboard within your ability level and obey posted signs and warnings.

Wear appropriate safety gear, including a helmet and goggles, to protect yourself from injury.

Stay hydrated and take regular breaks to rest and refuel throughout the day.

Be aware of changing weather conditions and dress in layers to stay warm and dry in the mountain environment.

Whether you're carving fresh tracks through powder-filled bowls, admiring panoramic views from the chairlift, or savoring après-ski delights in a cozy mountain lodge, a visit to Mount Erciyes Ski Resort promises an unforgettable winter adventure in the heart of Turkey's snow-capped mountains. So grab your gear, bundle up, and get ready to experience the thrill of the slopes in this alpine paradise.

Local Insights: Itineraries and Day Trip Recommendations from Locals

Who better to unveil the treasures of Cappadocia than those who call it home? Dive deep into the local experience with these insider itineraries and day trip recommendations crafted by residents themselves. From off-the-beaten-path attractions to hidden culinary gems, these recommendations promise to reveal the true essence of Cappadocia:

1. Serkan's Off-the-Beaten-Path Adventure:

Join Serkan, a seasoned local guide, on a journey to discover Cappadocia's hidden wonders. Start your day with a sunrise hike through the lesser-known valleys of Kılıçlar and Meskendir, where towering rock formations and ancient cave dwellings await. Afterward, visit the charming village of Mustafapaşa, known for its well-preserved Greek architecture and traditional stone houses. Cap off your adventure with a visit to the lesser-known Göreme Open-Air Museum, where fewer crowds mean more opportunities to explore the rock-cut churches and monasteries at your own pace.

2. Ayşe's Culinary Exploration:

Embark on a culinary journey with Ayşe, a passionate foodie and lifelong resident of Cappadocia. Start your day with a visit to the local market in Ürgüp, where you'll sample an array of fresh produce, spices, and artisanal products. Next, head to Avanos to try your hand at pottery making with a local artisan, followed by a traditional Turkish breakfast at a cozy village café. In the afternoon, indulge in a cooking class led by Ayşe herself, where you'll learn to prepare classic Cappadocian dishes such as mantı (Turkish dumplings) and testi kebabı (clay pot kebab), using locally sourced ingredients and time-honored recipes.

3. Mehmet's Cultural Immersion Tour:

Join Mehmet, a proud ambassador of Cappadocian culture, on a day of exploration and discovery. Begin your journey with a visit to the ancient town of Kaymaklı, where you'll explore the underground city and learn about its fascinating history dating back to the Hittite period. Next, immerse yourself in the local arts scene with a visit to a traditional carpet-weaving workshop in Ortahisar, followed by a performance of live music and dance at a local cultural center. End your day with a traditional Turkish dinner at Mehmet's favorite kebab house, where you'll savor the flavors of Cappadocia while swapping stories and sharing laughs with newfound friends.

4. Fatma's Nature Retreat:

Escape the hustle and bustle of the tourist trail with Fatma, a nature enthusiast and avid hiker. Begin your day with a sunrise hot air balloon ride over the fairy chimneys of Göreme, taking in panoramic views of the stunning landscape below. Afterward, embark on a guided hike through the picturesque valleys of Rose and Red, where you'll encounter hidden caves, panoramic viewpoints, and cascading waterfalls. Finish your day with a picnic lunch in the tranquil surroundings of Love Valley, surrounded by towering rock formations and blooming wildflowers.

With these insider itineraries and day trip recommendations from locals, you'll uncover the hidden gems and authentic experiences that make Cappadocia truly special. So lace up your hiking boots, pack your appetite, and get ready to embark on a journey of discovery in this enchanting region of Turkey.

Sustainable Tourism in Cappadocia

RESPONSIBLE TRAVEL PRACTICES

As travelers, we have the privilege of exploring the world's wonders, but with that privilege comes the responsibility to protect and preserve the destinations we visit. In Cappadocia, a region of unparalleled natural beauty and cultural heritage, adopting responsible travel practices is essential to ensure its longevity and safeguard its treasures for future generations. Here are some tips for practicing responsible travel in Cappadocia:

1. Respect the Environment:

Stay on designated trails when hiking or exploring natural areas to avoid damaging fragile ecosystems.

Dispose of waste properly and recycle whenever possible. Carry a reusable water bottle and refill it at designated refill stations to minimize plastic waste.

Avoid littering, and if you see trash on the trails or at tourist sites, consider picking it up and disposing of it properly.

2. Support Local Communities:

Choose locally owned accommodations, restaurants, and tour operators to support the local economy and promote sustainable tourism practices.

Respect the customs, traditions, and way of life of the local community. Learn a few basic phrases in Turkish and engage with locals in a respectful and friendly manner.

Purchase locally made souvenirs and handicrafts to support local artisans and preserve traditional craftsmanship.

3. Minimize Your Environmental Footprint:

Opt for eco-friendly transportation options such as walking, cycling, or using public transportation whenever possible.

Consider offsetting your carbon emissions from travel by supporting reputable carbon offset programs or initiatives that invest in renewable energy projects.

Conserve water and energy by taking shorter showers, turning off lights and air conditioning when not in use, and reusing towels and linens in accommodations.

4. Practice Responsible Photography:

Respect the privacy and cultural sensitivities of local residents when taking photos. Always ask for permission before photographing individuals, especially in rural or religious settings.

Avoid contributing to overtourism by being mindful of the impact of your photography on popular landmarks and attractions. Consider visiting lesser-known sites or exploring during off-peak times to minimize crowds.

5. Educate Yourself and Others:

Learn about the history, culture, and environmental issues facing Cappadocia before your visit. Understand the significance of the region's cultural heritage sites and natural landscapes.

Share your knowledge and experiences with fellow travelers, friends, and family, and encourage them to adopt responsible travel practices in Cappadocia and beyond.

Support organizations and initiatives that work to conserve and protect Cappadocia's cultural and natural heritage, whether through donations, volunteering, or advocacy efforts.

By embracing responsible travel practices, we can all play a part in preserving the beauty and integrity of Cappadocia for generations to come. Together, let's ensure that this magical region remains a source of wonder and inspiration for years to come.

ECO-FRIENDLY TOURS AND ACTIVITIES

For travelers seeking to explore the wonders of Cappadocia while minimizing their environmental impact, eco-friendly tours and activities offer a responsible and sustainable way to experience the region's natural beauty and cultural heritage. From hiking through pristine landscapes to supporting local conservation efforts, here are some eco-conscious options for exploring Cappadocia:

1. Guided Nature Walks and Hikes:

Embark on guided nature walks and hikes led by knowledgeable local guides who can offer insights into the region's flora, fauna, and geological formations. Choose trails that prioritize conservation and preservation, and opt for low-impact activities that allow you to immerse yourself in the natural beauty of

Cappadocia without disturbing fragile ecosystems.

2. Bicycle Tours and Rentals:

Explore Cappadocia's charming villages, scenic valleys, and historic landmarks on two wheels with a bicycle tour or rental. Cycling is a sustainable and eco-friendly way to travel, allowing you to cover more ground while minimizing your carbon footprint. Choose routes that take you off the beaten path and support locally owned businesses along the way.

3. Organic Farm Visits and Cooking Classes:

Gain insight into sustainable agriculture practices and traditional Turkish cuisine with a visit to an organic farm followed by a cooking class. Learn about organic farming methods, harvest fresh produce from the fields, and prepare delicious dishes using locally sourced ingredients.

Support farmers who prioritize environmental stewardship and sustainable food production.

4. Wildlife Watching and Birdwatching Tours:

Embark on wildlife watching and birdwatching tours to observe Cappadocia's diverse flora and fauna in their natural habitats. Keep an eye out for native species such as rock partridges, hoopoes, and wildflowers, and learn about the importance of preserving their habitats and ecosystems. Choose tour operators that adhere to responsible wildlife viewing practices and prioritize conservation efforts.

5. Cultural Heritage Conservation Tours:

Support local conservation efforts and learn about Cappadocia's rich cultural heritage with guided tours of historic sites, archaeological excavations, and cultural landmarks. Explore ancient rock-cut churches, underground cities, and traditional villages while gaining an understanding of the importance of preserving these sites for future generations. Contribute to conservation initiatives through donations or volunteer opportunities.

6. Responsible Hot Air Balloon Rides:

Experience the breathtaking beauty of Cappadocia from above with a hot air balloon ride that prioritizes safety, sustainability, and responsible tourism practices. Choose reputable operators that prioritize passenger safety, minimize noise pollution, and adhere to environmental regulations. Opt for smaller group sizes and early morning flights to reduce the impact on the environment and local communities.

7. Participate in Community-Based Tourism Initiatives:

Support community-based tourism initiatives that empower local residents and promote sustainable development in Cappadocia's rural areas. Stay in eco-friendly accommodations run by local families, participate in cultural exchange programs, and engage in activities that benefit the local community, such as volunteering or purchasing handmade crafts and souvenirs directly from artisans.

By choosing eco-friendly tours and activities in Cappadocia, travelers can minimize their environmental footprint, support local communities, and contribute to the conservation and preservation of this extraordinary region for generations to come. Let's explore responsibly and sustainably, ensuring that Cappadocia's natural and cultural heritage remains protected and cherished for years to come.

SUPPORTING LOCAL COMMUNITIES

In the heart of Cappadocia, where ancient traditions and modern aspirations converge, lies a network of vibrant communities eager to share their rich culture, heritage, and hospitality with visitors from around the world. By supporting local communities, travelers can contribute to sustainable development, economic empowerment, and cultural preservation in Cappadocia. Here's how you can make a positive impact and forge meaningful connections with the people who call this region home:

1. Choose Locally Owned Businesses:

Support the backbone of Cappadocia's economy by patronizing locally owned businesses, including accommodations, restaurants, shops, and tour operators. Opt for family-run guesthouses, boutique hotels, and traditional inns that offer authentic experiences and personalized service. By spending your money locally, you directly contribute to the livelihoods of residents and help sustain the local economy.

2. Participate in Community-Based Tourism:

Engage with local communities and immerse yourself in their way of life through community-based tourism initiatives. Stay in homestays or agriturismo accommodations hosted by local families, where you can experience traditional Turkish hospitality, sample home-cooked meals, and learn about local customs and traditions firsthand. Participate in cultural exchange programs, volunteer opportunities, and artisan workshops that foster meaningful connections and mutual understanding.

3. Support Artisans and Craftspeople:

Discover the exquisite craftsmanship of Cappadocia's artisans and craftspeople by purchasing handmade souvenirs, textiles, ceramics, and other traditional products directly from local markets, cooperatives, and workshops. Seek out opportunities to meet artisans, watch demonstrations of traditional techniques, and learn about the cultural significance of their craft. By supporting local artisans, you help preserve traditional craftsmanship and ensure the continuation of centuries-old traditions.

4. Attend Local Events and Festivals:

Celebrate the vibrant cultural heritage of Cappadocia by attending local events, festivals, and celebrations throughout the year. From traditional folk music and dance performances to culinary festivals and religious ceremonies, these events offer a glimpse into the region's diverse cultural tapestry and provide opportunities to engage with local communities. By participating in these festivities, you support cultural preservation efforts and promote community cohesion.

5. Respect Local Customs and Traditions:

Show respect for the customs, traditions, and beliefs of Cappadocia's residents by familiarizing yourself with local etiquette and cultural norms. Dress modestly when visiting religious sites, ask for permission before taking photographs of individuals, and observe local customs regarding greetings, gestures, and social interactions. By demonstrating cultural sensitivity and respect, you foster positive relationships with locals and promote cross-cultural understanding.

6. Leave a Positive Impact:

Be mindful of your environmental impact and strive to leave a positive footprint wherever you go. Dispose of waste responsibly, minimize water and energy consumption, and tread lightly in natural areas to preserve the region's pristine landscapes and biodiversity. Consider participating in volunteer activities such as community clean-up efforts, conservation projects, or educational initiatives that benefit local communities and contribute to sustainable development in Cappadocia.

By supporting local communities in Cappadocia, travelers can forge meaningful connections, enrich their travel experiences, and leave a lasting legacy of positive change in this extraordinary region. Together, let's empower communities, celebrate diversity, and foster a more sustainable and inclusive tourism industry in Cappadocia and beyond.

Local Insights: Sustainable Initiatives and Stories of Community Conservation Efforts

Additional Resources

MAPS OF CAPPADOCIA

When embarking on an adventure in Cappadocia, having a reliable map and understanding the region's geography can greatly enhance your experience. From exploring ancient rock-cut churches to hiking through scenic valleys, a well-prepared map can help you navigate Cappadocia's diverse landscapes and discover its hidden gems. Here's everything you need to know about maps of Cappadocia:

1. Detailed Road Maps:

Road maps of Cappadocia provide an overview of the region's highways, main roads, and secondary routes, making them indispensable for travelers exploring the area by car or bus. These maps typically include important landmarks, towns, and villages, as well as points of interest such as historic sites, viewpoints, and hiking trails. Look for maps that offer detailed information on road conditions, elevation changes, and distances between key destinations to help you plan your journey efficiently.

2. Topographic Maps:

Topographic maps offer a more detailed depiction of Cappadocia's terrain, including elevation contours, geological features, and natural landmarks. These maps are invaluable for hikers, cyclists, and outdoor enthusiasts seeking to explore the region's rugged landscapes on foot or by bike. Topographic maps can help you identify trails, locate scenic viewpoints, and navigate challenging terrain, allowing you to immerse yourself in Cappadocia's natural beauty with confidence.

3. Trail Maps and Hiking Guides:

For those venturing into Cappadocia's network of hiking trails, trail maps and hiking guides are essential tools for planning your route and navigating the terrain. These maps typically highlight popular hiking routes, loop trails, and multi-day treks, as well as points of interest along the way, such as rock-cut churches, cave dwellings, and panoramic viewpoints. Whether you're a seasoned hiker or a casual nature enthusiast, having a trail map can help you make the most of your outdoor adventures in Cappadocia.

4. Historical and Cultural Maps:

To delve deeper into Cappadocia's rich history and cultural heritage, consider using historical and cultural maps that highlight important landmarks, archaeological sites, and cultural attractions. These maps can guide you to ancient rock-cut churches, underground cities, and open-air museums, providing insights into the region's Byzantine past and UNESCO World Heritage sites. Use historical and cultural maps to plan immersive experiences that allow you to connect with Cappadocia's fascinating history and heritage.

5. Interactive Online Maps:

In addition to traditional paper maps, interactive online maps offer a convenient and dynamic way to explore Cappadocia from the comfort of your computer or mobile device. Websites and apps such as Google Maps, Maps.me, and AllTrails provide detailed maps of Cappadocia's trails, roads, and points of interest, along with real-time navigation and location-based services. Use these digital maps to plan your itinerary, find nearby amenities, and navigate Cappadocia's labyrinthine landscapes with ease.

Whether you're embarking on a road trip, setting out on a hiking adventure, or simply exploring the sights and sounds of Cappadocia's towns and villages, having the right maps and navigation tools at your disposal can help you make the most of your journey. So pack your map, chart your course, and get ready to discover the wonders of Cappadocia with confidence and curiosity.

Further Reading and Websites

For travelers eager to delve deeper into the rich history, culture, and natural beauty of Cappadocia, a wealth of resources awaits. From guidebooks and travelogues to informative websites and online forums, these sources offer invaluable insights and practical advice to help you plan your journey and make the most of your time in this enchanting region. Here are some recommended books, articles, and websites for further reading and exploration:

1. Guidebooks:

"Lonely Planet Turkey" by Lonely Planet: This comprehensive guidebook provides detailed information on Cappadocia's top attractions, accommodations, dining options, and outdoor activities, along with practical travel tips and cultural insights.

"Cappadocia: A Travel Guide to Turkey's Ancient Wonderland" by Jennifer Barclay: Offering a blend of travel narrative, historical background, and practical advice, this guidebook is ideal for travelers seeking a deeper understanding of Cappadocia's unique landscapes and cultural heritage.

2. Travelogues and Memoirs:

"Cappadocia" by Joy Stocke and Angie Brenner: Through vivid storytelling and stunning photography, this travelogue captures the essence of Cappadocia, weaving together personal anecdotes, historical context, and cultural observations to paint a vivid portrait of the region.

"Strolling Through Istanbul" by Hilary Sumner-Boyd and John Freely: While primarily focused on Istanbul, this classic travel memoir offers insights into Turkey's history, architecture, and culture, providing valuable context for understanding Cappadocia and its place within the broader Turkish landscape.

3. Online Resources:

Göreme National Park and the Rock Sites of Cappadocia (UNESCO): The official UNESCO website offers detailed information on Cappadocia's UNESCO World Heritage sites, including Göreme National Park and its rock-cut churches, cave dwellings, and geological formations.

Turkey Travel Planner: Founded by travel writer and Turkey expert Tom Brosnahan, this comprehensive website provides practical travel advice, destination guides, and resources for planning a trip to Cappadocia and other regions of Turkey.

4. Travel Blogs and Websites:

The Cappadocia Guide: This online travel guide offers comprehensive information on Cappadocia's attractions, activities, accommodations, and dining options, along with travel tips and recommendations from local experts.

Culture Trip: Explore Cappadocia's cultural heritage, culinary delights, and outdoor adventures through articles, guides, and curated travel experiences on Culture Trip's website.

5. Online Forums and Communities:

TripAdvisor Cappadocia Forum: Connect with fellow travelers, ask questions, and share advice and recommendations on TripAdvisor's Cappadocia forum, where members discuss everything from sightseeing tips to dining options and accommodation reviews.

Reddit: Join the r/Cappadocia subreddit to engage with a community of travelers, locals, and enthusiasts sharing stories, photos, and insights about Cappadocia and its attractions.

Whether you're seeking practical travel advice, historical context, or inspiration for your next adventure, these resources offer a wealth of information to enrich your exploration of Cappadocia. So dive in, immerse yourself in the stories and landscapes of this ancient wonderland, and prepare to embark on a journey of discovery unlike any other.

Traveler's Checklist

Before embarking on your journey to Cappadocia, it's essential to make sure you have everything you need for a smooth and enjoyable experience. From packing the right gear to organizing your travel documents, this traveler's checklist will help you prepare for your Cappadocia adventure:

1. Travel Documents:

Valid passport: Ensure your passport is valid for at least six months beyond your planned departure date.

Visa: Check if you need a visa to enter Turkey and apply for one if necessary. You can typically apply for an e-visa online before your trip.

Travel insurance: Consider purchasing travel insurance to cover medical emergencies, trip cancellations, and other unforeseen circumstances.

2. Accommodation and Transportation:

Accommodation bookings: Confirm your hotel or guesthouse reservations in advance, especially during peak tourist seasons.

Transportation arrangements: Arrange transportation to and from Cappadocia, whether by plane, bus, or car rental. If traveling by bus, consider booking tickets in advance, especially for long-distance routes.

3. Packing Essentials:

Clothing: Pack lightweight, breathable clothing suitable for exploring Cappadocia's varied landscapes. Include comfortable walking shoes, layers for cooler evenings, and a hat and sunglasses for sun protection.

Outdoor gear: If planning to hike or participate in outdoor activities, bring appropriate gear such as a daypack, water bottle, sunscreen, and insect repellent.

Camera and accessories: Capture the stunning scenery of Cappadocia with a camera or smartphone, along with extra batteries, memory cards, and a tripod for stable shots.

Universal adapter and chargers: Ensure you have the right adapters and chargers to keep your devices powered throughout your trip.

4. Health and Safety:

Prescription medications: Pack any necessary medications in their original containers, along with copies of your prescriptions.

First aid kit: Bring a basic first aid kit with essentials such as bandages, pain relievers, antiseptic wipes, and motion sickness medication.

Emergency contacts: Carry a list of emergency contacts, including local authorities, your embassy or consulate, and your travel insurance provider.

COVID-19 precautions: Check current travel restrictions, health guidelines, and vaccination requirements related to COVID-19 before your trip. Bring face masks, hand sanitizer, and disinfectant wipes for added safety.

5. Finances and Communication:

Currency: Exchange currency or withdraw Turkish lira (TRY) upon arrival in Turkey. ATMs are widely available in Cappadocia's major towns and cities.

Credit cards: Notify your bank of your travel plans and bring at least one major credit card for purchases and emergencies.

Communication: Consider purchasing a local SIM card or activating an international roaming plan for your mobile phone to stay connected during your trip.

6. Itinerary and Maps:

Itinerary: Plan your activities and sightseeing itinerary in advance, but leave room for flexibility and spontaneous discoveries.

Maps and guidebooks: Bring printed maps, guidebooks, or digital navigation tools to help you navigate Cappadocia's labyrinthine landscapes and find points of interest.

By checking off these essential items on your traveler's checklist, you'll be well-prepared to embark on a memorable adventure in Cappadocia, where ancient wonders and natural beauty await at every turn. So pack your bags, double-check your documents, and get ready to explore this extraordinary region of Turkey with confidence and excitement.

LOCAL INSIGHTS: INSIDER TIPS AND RESOURCES RECOMMENDED BY LOCALS

Who better to reveal the secrets of Cappadocia than those who call it home? From hidden hiking trails to off-the-beaten-path attractions, locals have a wealth of insider knowledge to share with adventurous travelers. Here are some insider tips and resources recommended by locals to help you make the most of your Cappadocia experience:

1. Hidden Gems and Lesser-Known Attractions:

Local hiking trails: Explore lesser-known hiking trails recommended by locals, such as the Red and Rose Valleys, Zemi Valley, or

Pigeon Valley, for stunning landscapes and fewer crowds.

Hidden rock-cut churches: Seek out lesser-known rock-cut churches and cave dwellings tucked away in remote valleys, away from the main tourist sites.

Secret viewpoints: Discover hidden viewpoints and panoramic vistas that offer uninterrupted views of Cappadocia's surreal landscapes, away from the crowds.

2. Authentic Dining Experiences:

Local eateries: Dine at authentic Turkish restaurants and local eateries favored by residents, where you can savor traditional dishes made with fresh, locally sourced ingredients.

Village breakfasts: Experience the joy of a traditional Turkish village breakfast, known as "köy kahvaltısı," featuring an array of fresh cheeses, olives, jams, and pastries.

3. Cultural Experiences and Workshops:

Artisan workshops: Participate in hands-on workshops led by local artisans, where you can learn traditional crafts such as pottery making, carpet weaving, and ceramics painting.

Cultural events: Attend local festivals, music performances, and cultural events to immerse yourself in Cappadocia's vibrant arts scene and connect with the local community.

4. Insider Resources and Recommendations:

Local guides and tour operators: Hire knowledgeable local guides or join small-group tours led by experts who can provide insider insights and personalized recommendations.

Community-run initiatives: Support community-based tourism initiatives and social enterprises that empower local residents and promote sustainable development in Cappadocia.

5. Online Communities and Forums:

Social media groups: Join Facebook groups or online forums dedicated to Cappadocia travel, where locals and travelers share tips, recommendations, and insider advice.

Instagram accounts: Follow local influencers and photographers on Instagram who showcase Cappadocia's beauty and share insider tips on hidden spots and unique experiences.

6. Off-Peak Travel:

Visit during shoulder seasons: Consider traveling to Cappadocia during the shoulder seasons of spring (April to June) and autumn (September to November) to avoid crowds and enjoy milder weather.

Early morning and late afternoon visits: Explore popular attractions such as Göreme Open-Air Museum or watch the sunrise from a hot air balloon for a quieter and more peaceful experience.

By tapping into the wisdom and expertise of locals, you'll uncover hidden treasures, discover authentic experiences, and forge meaningful connections with the people and places of Cappadocia. So don't be afraid to ask for recommendations, follow your curiosity, and embrace the spirit of adventure as you explore this extraordinary region of Turkey.

Printed in Great Britain
by Amazon